The Gen **X** Series

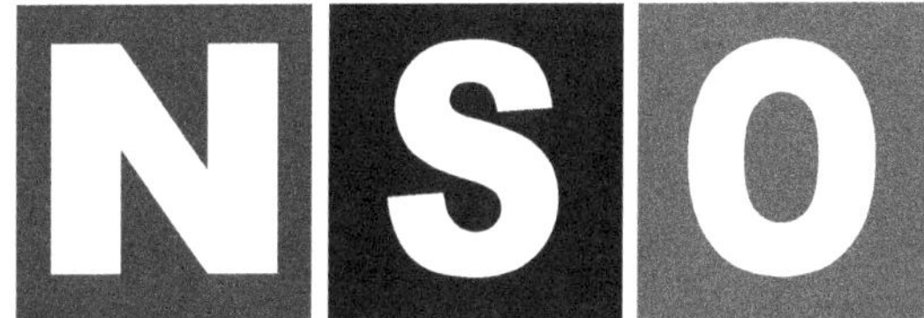

NSO

OLYMPIAD WORKBOOK

3

NATIONAL SCIENCE OLYMPIAD

01 Learning Objectives

02 Multiple Choice Questions

03 HOTS (Achievers Section)

04 Model Test Paper

05 Answer Keys and Solutions

06 OMR Answer Sheet

V&S PUBLISHERS

Published by:

V&S PUBLISHERS

F-2/16, Ansari road, Daryaganj, New Delhi-110002
☎ 23240026, 23240027 • *Fax:* 011-23240028
✉ info@vspublishers.com • 🌐 www.vspublishers.com

Online Brandstore: amazon.in/vspublishers

Regional Office : Hyderabad

5-1-707/1, Brij Bhawan (Beside Central Bank of India Lane)
Bank Street, Koti, Hyderabad - 500 095
☎ 040-24737290
✉ vspublishershyd@gmail.com

Follow us on:   

BUY OUR BOOKS FROM: | AMAZON | | FLIPKART |

© Copyright: **V&S PUBLISHERS**
ISBN 978-81-977761-2-0
New Edition

PUBLISHER'S NOTE

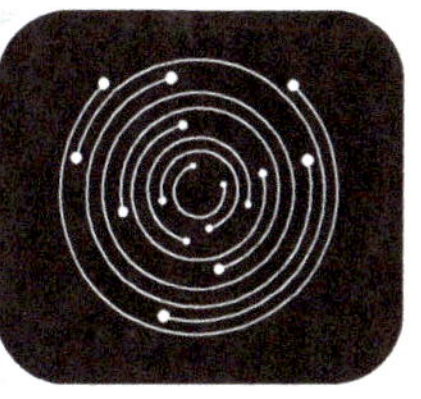

V&S Publishers has carved a significant niche in the publishing industry over the last decade, having successfully published more than 1000 titles across 9 languages spanning over 50 subject categories. Being known for the quality of content, we have built a reputation of excellence and reliability. We have consistently delivered **"Value & Substance"** to our readers, through a wide range of titles across a variety of genres covering school books, fiction and non-fiction that caters to different people from every section of the society.

The **Olympiad Guidebooks for classes 1-10** across all subjects, launched almost a decade ago, under the **GEN X Imprint**, became a go-to-source for the school students in no time, owing to their invaluable and substantive content written in a guidebook pattern,.

Having successfully sold a million copies of the same and in response to demand by both students as well as shopkeepers nationwide; we now present before you our newly launched **Olympiad Workbook Series**, designed for **classes 1-10 across 4 subjects**.

The workbooks are meticulously curated by a team of experienced educators, researchers and subject matter experts, edited by professionals and peer reviewed by teachers. The team has poured its efforts and expertise into creating a crisp and concise workbook which will help and guide the students to the path of success in Olympiad exams. The **MCQs** identified will not only help in scoring top marks in Olympiads but also inculcate a sense of deeper understanding of the subject, by way of solving **HOTS** and referring to complete solutions at the end of the book.

Here we present our new release– **OLYMPIAD WORKBOOK (NSO) CLASS–3** having following features:

☞ Based on the latest syllabi

☞ MCQs with comprehensive coverage of topics

☞ HOTS Questions liberally included

☞ A dedicated chapter on logical reasoning

☞ Model test paper for thorough practice

☞ Sample OMR sheet for real time simulation

We have made sure through our best efforts, that this workbook strictly follows the latest syllabi and patterns of the Olympiad Examination.

As **V&S Publishers** continuously strive to enhance the readability and maintain the credibility of our academic publications, we seek the support of our valuable readers in influencing and enriching the lives of future generations of students.

P.S. While every care has been taken to ensure the correctness of the content, if you come across any error, howsoever minor, do not hesitate to discuss with teachers while pointing that out to us in no uncertain terms.

We wish you all the best for your exams!

DISTINCTIVE FEATURES

01 — Learning Objectives

They list the whole chapter as subtopics, helping the teachers to guide children in a step-by-step manner.

02 — Multiple Choice Questions

MCQs act as an excellent learning aid, helping you to understand and work on your mistakes.

03 — HOTS (Achievers Section)

The High Order Thinking Questions aim to help the student to solve Application-based questions and gain practical understanding of the subject.

04 — Model Test Paper

Model test paper are provided at the end of each book, which help the student to test the knowledge which they have gained after thorough reading of all chapters.

05 — Answer Key

Detailed Answer Key along with explanations aid the pupil to indentify, understand the mistakes they make during the course of Olympiad preparation.

CONTENTS

Chapter 1 : Plants and Animals 7

Chapter 2 : Birds 11

Chapter 3 : Food 15

Chapter 4 : Housing, Clothing and Occupation 18

Chapter 5 : Transport and Communication 22

Chapter 6 : Human Body 26

Chapter 7 : Earth and Universe 30

Chapter 8 : Matter and Materials 34

Chapter 9 : Light, Force and Sound 39

Chapter 10 : Our environment 43

Chapter 11 : Logical Reasoning 45

Model Test Paper **50**

Hints and Solutions **54**

PLANTS AND ANIMALS

LEARNING OBJECTIVES

- ➤ Plants
- ➤ Animals
- ➤ The food chain
- ➤ Different parts of a plant
- ➤ Different types of animals
- ➤ How animals eat

MULTIPLE CHOICE QUESTIONS

1. Plants get carbon dioxide from _________.
   (A) Air
   (B) Leaves
   (C) Soil
   (D) Sand

2. The main purpose of a plant's flower is to _________.
   (A) Provide support
   (B) Provide water
   (C) Produce food
   (D) Produce seed

3. Name the green colouring substance that is present in leaves.
   (A) Salt
   (B) Carotene
   (C) Chlorophyll
   (D) All of these

4. This part of a root helps with absorption _________.
   (A) Guard cells
   (B) Root hairs
   (C) Phloem
   (D) Stems

5. Which of the following is a plant whose stem can be upright only with a support?
   (A) Rose
   (B) Watermelon
   (C) Moneyplant
   (D) Mango

6. Which of these is not needed for photosynthesis?
   (A) Chlorophyll
   (B) Sunlight
   (C) Oxygen
   (D) Water

7. Which part of a plant soaks up water and minerals and stores food also.
   (A) Root
   (B) Leaves
   (C) Flowers
   (D) Stem

8. Which gas do plants release into the air?
   (A) Oxygen
   (B) Hydrogen
   (C) Carbon dioxide
   (D) Nitrogen

9. _________ hold the seeds.
   (A) Roots
   (B) Leaves
   (C) Stems
   (D) Fruits

10. Which statement is not true?
    (A) A plant comes from a seed.
    (B) Leaves are attached to the stem.
    (C) Roots of a plant are usually above the soil.
    (D) A plant is a living thing that grows.

11. A plant needs _________ to survive.
    (A) Food, clothing, electricity
    (B) Water, silver, oil, and a place to grow
    (C) Air, shelter, gold
    (D) Food, water, air, light and a place to grow

12. Plants that get energy from the food they make are called _________.
    (A) Herbivores
    (B) Producers
    (C) Omnivores
    (D) Carnivores

13. Several seeds are planted on a hill. Which of the following growths will you see first?
   (A) A tree   (B) A bush
   (C) A seedling   (D) Roots

14. ________ trees stay green all year round.
   (A) Pine   (B) Oak
   (C) Maple   (D) Evergreen

15. ________ trees lose their leaves in the fall or autumn.
   (A) Deciduous   (B) Pine
   (C) Evergreen   (D) Herbivore

16. A tiger is a ________.
   (A) Carnivore   (B) Herbivore
   (C) Omnivore   (D) Dinosaur

17. Omnivores eat ________.
   (A) Seak
   (B) Carrot sticks
   (C) Plants and animals
   (D) Animals

18. What is a food chain?
   (A) The relationship an animal has with everything around them
   (B) A grocery store
   (C) A group of bigger animals that eat smaller ones
   (D) None of these

19. Which of the following animals chews cud?
   (A) Ducks   (B) Monkeys
   (C) Cows   (D) Snakes

20. How do snakes eat their food?
   (A) With a knife and fork
   (B) In tiny pieces
   (C) By swallowing in whole
   (D) Through a straw

21. Find the odd one among the following animals.
   (A) Ant   (B) Frog
   (C) Grasshopper   (D) Cockroach

22. Whose job is it to protect wild animals and their forest home?

   (A) goat
   (B) colobus monkey
   (C) building
   (D) mine

23. The main role of a producer is ________.
   (A) To kill animals
   (B) To eat other animals
   (C) To get eaten by eagles
   (D) To prepare food

24. Frogs depend on ________ for their food.
   (A) Grass   (B) Snakes
   (C) Other frogs   (D) Grasshopper

25. Which of the following sucks blood from other animals with the help of suckers?
   (A) Butterflies   (B) Spiders
   (C) Leech   (D) Mushroom

26. The long tongue of the butterflies is called ________.
   (A) Sucker   (B) Gill
   (C) Stomata   (D) Proboscis

27. Study the following chart:

Plants	→	X	→	Lion

   The arrow means "is eaten by". Which of the following animals can X be?
   (A) Frog   (B) Eagle
   (C) Goat   (D) Snake

28. Which of the following animals has no teeth to tear food?
   (A) Cat   (B) Dog
   (C) Cow   (D) Lion

OLYMPIAD WORKBOOK (NSO) CLASS–3

29. Which animal is used to make wool?
(A) Sheep   (B) Leopard
(C) Goat   (D) Lion

30. Which of the following spins webs to trap insects and eat them?
(A) Butterflies   (B) Honey bees
(C) Fire flies   (D) Spiders

HOTS (ACHIEVERS SECTION)

31. In a pond, 1/8 of the animals are amphibians, 1/8 are mammals, 2/8 are fish, and 3/8 are insects. The remaining animals are reptiles. Choose the correct option that shows a subtraction equation 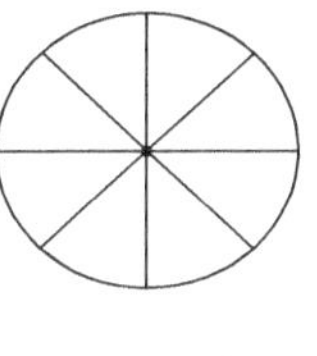 with the fraction of animals in the pond, which are reptiles.

(A) $8/8 - 7/8 = 1/8$
(B) $8/8 - 1/8 - 1/8 - 2/8 - 3/8 = 1/8$
(C) $8/8 - 1/8 - 1/8 - 3/8 - 2/8 = 1/8$
(D) Both (A) and (B) are correct

32. The graph below shows information about different animals.

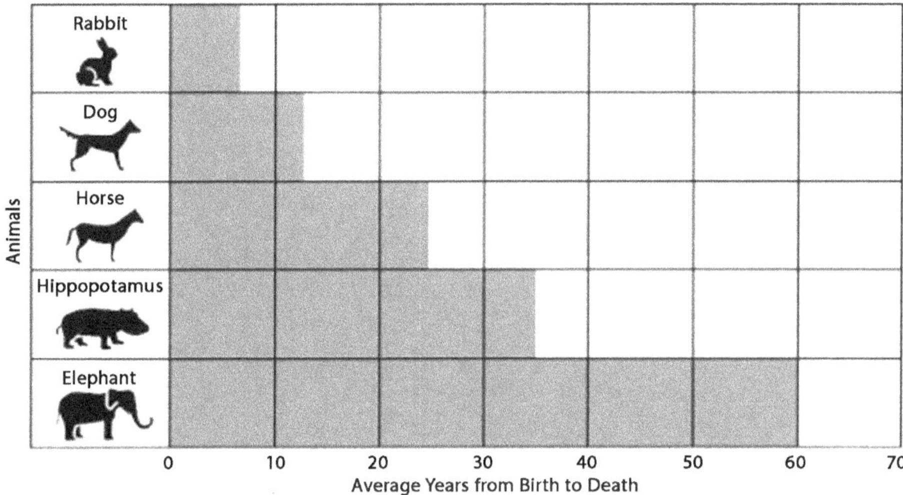

I. Select the best title for this graph.
II. Which animal(s) is/are herbivores?

	I	II
(A)	Life cycle of some animals	Elephant
(B)	Life span of some animals	Rabbit, elephant and hippopotamus
(C)	Life processes of some animals	Hippopotamus and dog
(D)	Life functions of some animals	Dog and elephant

33. Look at the plant shown below.

Which of the following correctly describes the function of the parts labelled X and Y?

	X	Y
(A)	Makes food for the plant	Supports branches and leaves
(B)	Makes food for the plant	Absorbs nutrients and water from soil
(C)	Absorbs nutrients and water from soil	Makes food for the plant
(D)	Has different shapes and edges	Absorbs nutrients and water from soil

34. Which of the following is not a disease of plants?
    (A) Red striped disease
    (B) Banana wilt
    (C) Cotton wool disease
    (D) Leaf rust

35. Which of the following functions of teeth is correctly matched?
    (A) Canines   (i)   Bite food
    (B) Incisors   (ii) Tear food
    (C) Broad back teeth (iii) Chewing cud
    (D) Wisdom tooth   (iv) Gnaw food

BIRDS

MULTIPLE CHOICE QUESTIONS

1. Birds change the direction of their flight using _________.
   - (A) Down feather
   - (B) Flight feather
   - (C) Tail feather
   - (D) Breast bone

2. Which of the following can fly for great distances?
   - (A) Kiwi
   - (B) Penguin
   - (C) Eagle
   - (D) Peacock

3. Which of the following has sharp eyes to see its prey on the ground?
   - (A) Hen
   - (B) Eagle
   - (C) Crane
   - (D) Duck

4. Which of the following has webbed feet?
   - (A) Duck
   - (B) Peacock
   - (C) Hen
   - (D) Parrot

5. Which of the following is a wading bird?
   - (A) Sparrow
   - (B) Hen
   - (C) Crane
   - (D) Eagle

6. Which of the following bird makes a nest on the ground from pebbles and stones?
   - (A) Hen
   - (B) Pigeon
   - (C) Eagle
   - (D) Penguin

7. Which of the following statement is/are correct about birds?
   - (A) All birds can fly.
   - (B) Most birds lay eggs, while some give birth to their young ones.
   - (C) All birds have an outer covering of feathers.
   - (D) Both (A) and (C)

8. The feathers of a bird _________.
   - (A) Keep it warm
   - (B) Help it in flying
   - (C) Protect the body
   - (D) All of the above

9. Select the incorrect match(es) between the bird and the claw.
   - (A)   Eagle
   - (B)   Crow
   - (C)   Ostrich
   - (D) Both (A) and (B)

10. Which of these birds uses its beak as a needle to sew leaves with materials like thread and wool?
    (A) Tailor bird
    (B) Weaver bird
    (C) Woodpecker
    (D) None of these
11. During the upstroke _________.
    (A) The wings of the bird do not move.
    (B) The wings of the bird move upward.
    (C) The wings of the bird move downward.
    (D) The tail of the bird change direction.
12. Which of the following is a water bird?
    (A) Sparrow   (B) Crane
    (C) Eagle   (D) Peacock
13. A bird is different from a bat because _________.
    (A) It can fly
    (B) It has feathers
    (C) It can grow
    (D) It needs air
14. Which of the following birds has special oil glands that make its feathers waterproof?
    (A) Duck   (B) Eagle
    (C) Sparrow   (D) Hen
15. Which of the following can run the fastest?
    (A) Penguin   (B) Eagle
    (C) Sparrow   (D) Parrot
16. Which of the following is a perching bird?
    (A) Crow   (B) Parrot
    (C) Penguin   (D) Duck
17. A woodpecker has two toes in the front and two toes in the back. It is a _________.
    (A) Climbing bird
    (B) Perching bird
    (C) Preying bird
    (D) Swimming bird
18. Identify the preying bird from the following.
    (A) Parrot   (B) Sparrow
    (C) Eagle   (D) Crane
19. Which kind of birds can run and walk on the ground?
    (A) Scratching bird   (B) Wading bird
    (C) Swimming bird   (D) Perching bird
20. Scratching birds have _________.
    (A) Three toes in front and one short toe at the back with sharp claws
    (B) Thin, long legs with spreading toes
    (C) Webbed feet with skin between their toes
    (D) Two toes pointing upward and two toes pointing downwards
21. A woodpecker has _________.
    (A) Chisel-shaped, strong and heavy beak
    (B) Broad, flat beak with strainers
    (C) Broad, long and pointed beak
    (D) Long, slender and curved beak

22. Which of the following is an incorrect match?

Option	Name of bird	Habitat	Beak (Purpose)	Feet (Purpose)
(A)	Ostrich	Trees	Drilling holes	Climbing
(B)	Hummingbird	Meadows	Probing (nectar)	Perching
(C)	Eagle	Trees	Catching insects	Perching
(D)	Woodpecker	Open land, prairie	Filtering	Running

23. This claw belongs to __________.

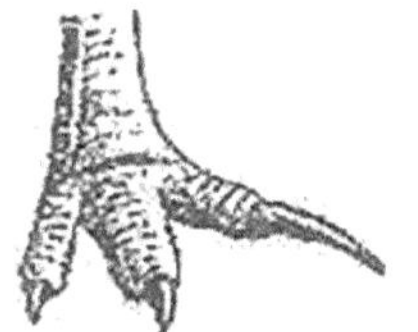

(A) Swimmers   (B) Waders
(C) Runners   (D) Perchers

24. This pair of feet belongs to __________.

(A) Swimmers   (B) Waders
(C) Runners   (D) Perchers

25. This beak belongs to __________.

(A) A robin
(B) A sparrow
(C) A woodpecker
(D) A quail

26. Seed-eaters like sparrows and cardinals have short, thick conical bills for cracking seed. This is a physical feature of __________.

(A) Cracker   (B) Shredder
(C) Chisel   (D) Tweezer

27. A beak like a knife is good for __________.
(A) Stabbing at food
(B) Filter things out of water
(C) Cutting through meat
(D) Breaking open hard shells

28. Identify the bird: __________.

(A) Flamingo
(B) Bee-eater
(C) Scarlet ibis
(D) Common nighthawk

29. Sleeping habits can also change with __________.
(A) The seasons   (B) The region
(C) The weather   (D) The bird

30. __________ hammer to attract mates, to establish and defend territories, to excavate nesting sites, and to search for insects.
(A) Robin   (B) Sparrow
(C) Eagle   (D) Woodpeckers

HOTS (ACHIEVERS SECTION)

31. Why don't the birds fall when they sleep on the branch of a tree?
(A) Because of the shape of their claws that hold on to the branch very firmly.
(B) Birds do not sleep on the branches, they sleep in their nests.
(C) Because their feathers balance their weight.
(D) None of these

32. What's the easiest way to tell the difference between wading birds and perching birds?
  (A) Difference in wingspan
  (B) Difference in body size
  (C) Difference in foot structure
  (D) Difference in eyes
33. Which of the following birds has webbed feet?
  (A) Duck
  (B) Eagle
  (C) Hen
  (D) Pigeon
34. Which of the following senses is weakest in birds?
  (A) Hearing
  (B) Sight
  (C) Smell
  (D) Touch
35. What are the advantages of cone shaped beak?
  (A) It is easy to sip nectar from them.
  (B) It is easy to kill the fish with it.
  (C) It makes the beak strong and is used for cracking seeds.
  (D) It is easy to catch the prey.

1.	A B C D	8.	A B C D	15.	A B C D	22	A B C D	29.	A B C D
2.	A B C D	9.	A B C D	16.	A B C D	23.	A B C D	30.	A B C D
3.	A B C D	10.	A B C D	17.	A B C D	24.	A B C D	31.	A B C D
4.	A B C D	11.	A B C D	18.	A B C D	25.	A B C D	32.	A B C D
5.	A B C D	12.	A B C D	19.	A B C D	26.	A B C D	33.	A B C D
6.	A B C D	13.	A B C D	20.	A B C D	27.	A B C D	34.	A B C D
7.	A B C D	14.	A B C D	21.	A B C D	28.	A B C D	35.	A B C D

FOOD

LEARNING OBJECTIVES

➤ Plants and animals as sources of food
➤ Classifing food into energy giving, body building and protective
➤ Identifing various nutrients present in food

MULTIPLE CHOICE QUESTIONS

1. Which of these would give you energy?
   (A) Glucose (B) Milk
   (C) Butter parantha (D) All of these

2. Protein is found in _________.
   (A) Meat (B) Orange
   (C) Cucumber (D) Asparagus

3. Which of the following falls in the category of protective food?
   (A) Wheat (B) Rice
   (C) Sugar (D) Oranges

4. Tomato belongs to which category of food?
   (A) Vegetable (B) Fruit
   (C) Cereal (D) Pulses

5. Which of the following grows under-ground?
   (A) Potato (B) Onion
   (C) Garlic (D) All of these

6. Read the given statements and find out the incorrect one.
   (A) Vitamin A is found in darkly coloured red, orange or yellow vegetables and fruits.
   (B) Rice, wheat, ragi, bajra, maize, jowar, barley, rice flakes, wheat flour: all are sources of carbohydrates.
   (C) Milk protein is of good quality, and this is why milk is considered good for children.
   (D) Flesh foods include only meat and fish.

7. Which of the following are sources of energy?
   (A) Meat group
   (B) Fats, oils and sweets
   (C) Breads and cereals
   (D) Milk and cheese

8. Which of these is not considered a nutrient?
   (A) Vitamins (B) Minerals
   (C) Fibre (D) Fats

9. Which of these is added to the food label so that people sometimes don't eat it in excess?
   (A) Fat (B) Calcium
   (C) Sodium (D) Cholesterol

10. Which of these is required to be on the food label?
    (A) Total carbohydrate (B) Sugars
    (C) Iron (D) All of these

11. The bread, cereal, rice and pasta are good sources of _________.
    (A) Carbohydrate (B) Vitamin C
    (C) Calcium (D) Vitamin D

12. Citrus fruits are an excellent source of __________.
    (A) Calcium   (B) Vitamin C
    (C) Vitamin B   (D) Calories
13. Meat, poultry, fish, dry beans, eggs and nuts are an important source of __________.
    (A) Protein   (B) Fibre
    (C) Beta carotene   (D) Calcium
14. Which of the following has highest quantity of fat?
    (A) Graham crackers (B) Brownies
    (C) Pudding   (D) Angel food cake
15. Milk, cheese and yogurt are important for __________.
    (A) Strong bones   (B) Teeth
    (C) Muscles   (D) All of these
16. How many servings of vegetables do we need each day?
    (A) 6–11   (B) 2–3
    (C) 3–5   (D) 1–2
17. According to the Food Guide Pyramid, you should eat the maximum servings in a day from which of the following food groups?
    (A) Vegetables
    (B) Milk, yogurt, and cheese
    (C) Bread, cereal, rice, and pasta
    (D) Meat, poultry, fish and beans
18. Recommended daily servings for teenage boys as compared with teenage girls __________.
    (A) Are larger for most food groups.
    (B) Are smaller for the milk group and larger for all other groups.
    (C) Are the same for all food groups.
    (D) Are larger for the meat group and the same for all other groups.
19. Which of the following foods is a good source of fibre?
    (A) A piece of pie
    (B) Scrambled eggs
    (C) Potato skin
    (D) A cup of yogurt
20. Which of the following foods contains unsaturated fat?
    (A) Cheese   (B) Butter
    (C) Steak   (D) Olive oil

21. Which of the following is not a recommended way to get the nutrients you need?
    (A) Skipping meals
    (B) Eliminate foods from the tip of the pyramid from your diet.
    (C) Watch portion sizes
    (D) Balanced intake of nutrients.
22. An average teen should eat __________.
    (A) Not more than 1,500 calories a day
    (B) About 1,200 calories a meal
    (C) Between 2,000 and 2,500 calories a day
    (D) Between 3,000 and 3,200 calories a day
23. A person who does not eat meat should __________.
    (A) Eat less of milk products.
    (B) Substitute pasta for meat.
    (C) Eat additional servings of carbohydrates, fats and proteins.
    (D) Substitute it with beans, eggs, and nuts.
24. Which of the following is important for strong muscles, bones and teeth?
    (A) Vitamins   (B) Calcium
    (C) Fats   (D) Lactose
25. Which of the following is a recommended way to remain healthy?
    (A) Eating a balanced diet.
    (B) Eating foods high in fats and calories.
    (C) Taking too much sugar.
    (D) Taking excess salt in the diet.
26. Skimmed milk does not contain which of the following?
    (A) Calcium   (B) Fat
    (C) Protein   (D) Vitamin B2
27. Which of the following can be a substitute for milk?
    (A) Cereal
    (B) Leafy vegetables
    (C) Pulses
    (D) Cheese
28. Sprouting of cereals helps in improving the content of: __________
    (A) Vitamin A   (B) Vitamin B
    (C) Vitamin C   (D) Protein

29. Pulses are a major source of: _________
   (A) Proteins   (B) Vitamin C
   (C) Carbohydrates   (D) Vitamin D
30. In order to improve the vitamin C content of pulses, we must: _________

   (A) Ferment them
   (B) Combine them with vegetables
   (C) Mix them with cereals
   (D) Sprout them

HOTS (ACHIEVERS SECTION)

31. We can have vitamins and minerals if we eat ______.
   (A) Vegetables
   (B) Fruits
   (C) Protective foods
   (D) All of these
32. Select the cooking method which is different from the other three.
   (A) Roasting chapati
   (B) Boiling rice
   (C) Steaming momos
   (D) Frying puri
33. Read the given statements.
   i.   Cooking makes the food soft, tasty and easy to chew and digest.
   ii. Reheating food again and again restores nutrients in the food.
   iii. Eating junk food very often can lead to health problems.
   iv. Old people need food that is hard and raw.

   Which of these statements is/are INCORRECT?

   (A) i, ii and iii only   (B) iii and iv only
   (C) ii and iv only   (D) iii only
34. Select the correct option to fill the empty boxes of the given flowchart.

   We eat the stem of

   [ ] — Ginger — [ ]

   (A) Turnip and Radish
   (B) Sugarcane and Carrot
   (C) Turnip and Spinach
   (D) Potato and Sugarcane
35. Select the correct statement.
   (A) Roughage present in vegetables and fruits must be discarded.
   (B) Overcooking decreases the nutritive value of food.
   (C) Preserved food has conditions suitable for growth of microbes.
   (D) Growing children need more fats to build strong muscles.

—Darken Your Choice with HB Pencil —

1.	Ⓐ Ⓑ Ⓒ Ⓓ	8.	Ⓐ Ⓑ Ⓒ Ⓓ	15.	Ⓐ Ⓑ Ⓒ Ⓓ	22	Ⓐ Ⓑ Ⓒ Ⓓ	29.	Ⓐ Ⓑ Ⓒ Ⓓ
2.	Ⓐ Ⓑ Ⓒ Ⓓ	9.	Ⓐ Ⓑ Ⓒ Ⓓ	16.	Ⓐ Ⓑ Ⓒ Ⓓ	23.	Ⓐ Ⓑ Ⓒ Ⓓ	30.	Ⓐ Ⓑ Ⓒ Ⓓ
3.	Ⓐ Ⓑ Ⓒ Ⓓ	10.	Ⓐ Ⓑ Ⓒ Ⓓ	17.	Ⓐ Ⓑ Ⓒ Ⓓ	24.	Ⓐ Ⓑ Ⓒ Ⓓ	31.	Ⓐ Ⓑ Ⓒ Ⓓ
4.	Ⓐ Ⓑ Ⓒ Ⓓ	11.	Ⓐ Ⓑ Ⓒ Ⓓ	18.	Ⓐ Ⓑ Ⓒ Ⓓ	25.	Ⓐ Ⓑ Ⓒ Ⓓ	32.	Ⓐ Ⓑ Ⓒ Ⓓ
5.	Ⓐ Ⓑ Ⓒ Ⓓ	12.	Ⓐ Ⓑ Ⓒ Ⓓ	19.	Ⓐ Ⓑ Ⓒ Ⓓ	26.	Ⓐ Ⓑ Ⓒ Ⓓ	33.	Ⓐ Ⓑ Ⓒ Ⓓ
6.	Ⓐ Ⓑ Ⓒ Ⓓ	13.	Ⓐ Ⓑ Ⓒ Ⓓ	20.	Ⓐ Ⓑ Ⓒ Ⓓ	27.	Ⓐ Ⓑ Ⓒ Ⓓ	34.	Ⓐ Ⓑ Ⓒ Ⓓ
7.	Ⓐ Ⓑ Ⓒ Ⓓ	14.	Ⓐ Ⓑ Ⓒ Ⓓ	21.	Ⓐ Ⓑ Ⓒ Ⓓ	28.	Ⓐ Ⓑ Ⓒ Ⓓ	35.	Ⓐ Ⓑ Ⓒ Ⓓ

HOUSING, CLOTHING AND OCCUPATION

LEARNING OBJECTIVES

➤ Different types of houses
➤ Clothes and fibers
➤ Different occupations

MULTIPLE CHOICE QUESTIONS

1. Which one is a permanent house?
   (A) Igloo   (B) Tent
   (C) Bungalow   (D) Caravan

2. Which is a stronger house?
   (A) Multi-storey building
   (B) Igloo
   (C) Stilted house
   (D) House boat

3. A house protects us from _______.
   (A) Heat   (B) Cold
   (C) Wild animals   (D) All of these

4. A stilt house is made up of _______.
   (A) Bricks
   (B) Mud
   (C) Straw
   (D) Bamboo and wood

5. An igloo is a temporary house made by _______.

   (A) Eskimos   (B) Red indians
   (C) Africans   (D) Arabs

6. Spruce is a light _______.
   (A) Low-density wood
   (B) High-density wood
   (C) Low-density plastic
   (D) High-density plastic

7. Sunlight keeps the rooms dry and free from _______.
   (A) Germs   (B) Dogs
   (C) Cats   (D) Rats

8. Which of the following is harmful to our health?
   (A) Eating fresh, warm and clean food.
   (B) Washing our hands before eating food.
   (C) Swallowing the food without chewing it.
   (D) Eating regularly at the same time of the day.

9. Which of the following rooms is used for cooking food in our home?
   (A) Bathroom   (B) Kitchen
   (C) Bedroom   (D) Balcony

10. Straw, bamboo, leaves and mud are the main components to construct which type of house?
    (A) Kutcha house   (B) Tent house
    (C) Bungalow   (D) Skyscrapers

11. Concrete is a paste containing _______.
    (A) Cement, sand and crushed rock
    (B) Cement and crushed rock
    (C) Cement, sand and water
    (D) Sand and crushed rock

OLYMPIAD WORKBOOK (NSO) CLASS – 3

12. Which among the following are protein fibres?
    (A) Cotton and silk
    (B) Cotton and linen
    (C) Nylon and wool
    (D) Wool and silk
13. Oak is a type of _______.
    (A) Wood
    (B) Metal
    (C) Building material
    (D) Both (A) and (C)
14. Who am I?
    (i) I can mend chappals and shoes.
    (ii) You can find me sitting by the roadside or some time inside the shoes.
    (A) Sweeper   (B) Cobbler
    (C) Postman   (D) Policeman
15. Which of the following fabrics does not take stains easily?
    (A) Cotton   (B) Nylon
    (C) Wool   (D) Silk
16. Which of the following fabrics is a bad conductor?
    (A) Nylon   (B) Wool
    (C) Rayon   (D) Cotton
17. Which fabric is made of staple fiber?
    (A) Cotton   (B) Nylon
    (C) Polyester   (D) Silk
18. Which is the strongest fiber?
    (A) Cotton   (B) Nylon
    (C) Rayon   (D) Wool
19. Which fabric has a dull surface?
    (A) Nylon   (B) Polyester
    (C) Silk   (D) Wool
20. Cotton is most desirable fabric for making undergarments because it is _______.
    (A) Absorbant   (B) Dull
    (C) Shinning   (D) Strong
21. Denim is a fabric which is _______.
    (A) Light weight and loosely woven
    (B) Transparent and crisp
    (C) Heavy weight and thick
    (D) Medium weight and plain
22. Clothes are made from _______.

    (A) Fibers   (B) Microbes
    (C) Plants   (D) Animals
23. Ananya's mother told her to wear dark clothes in winter. Why?
    (A) They look nice
    (B) They look fashionable
    (C) They absorb heat from the atmosphere
    (D) They look cozy
24. Which type of clothes are best suited for rainy season?
    (A) Cotton   (B) Polyester
    (C) Linen   (D) Woolen
25. Woolen clothes are prepared from _______.
    (A) Cotton plant
    (B) Wool of sheep
    (C) Wool worns
    (D) Carbon compounds
26. Silk clothes are prepared from _______.
    (A) Silk flies   (B) Silk plant
    (C) Silk worm   (D) Sheep
27. Choose the correct option and select the correct answer.

	Occupation		Tools used
a.	Architect	i.	Pliers
b.	Carpenter	ii.	Drill
c.	Electrician	iii.	Compass
d.	Mechanic	iv.	Hammer

    (A) a-i, b-iv, c-iii, d-ii
    (B) a-iii, b-i, c-iv, d-ii
    (C) a-ii, b-iv, c-i, d- iii
    (D) a-iii, b-iv, c-i, d-ii
28. Match the following and choose the correct option.
    I. This person makes layouts for buildings.
    II. A doctor uses this instrument to check your heartbeat.

	I	II
(A)	Doctor	Drill
(B)	Architect	Stethoscope
(C)	Engineer	Stethoscope
(D)	Doctor	Thermometer

29. Match the following and choose the correct option.
   I.   What is the work of an electrician?
   II. A gardener used a spade to do this job.

	I	II
(A)	Taking care of houses	Decorate
(B)	Making buildings	Dig
(C)	Repairs electrical appliances	Dig
(D)	Repairs electrical appliances	Decorate

30. Whom will you call to get the following repaired in your houses? Choose the correct option.

	I	II
a.	A leak tap	i. Painter
b.	A broken wooden chair	ii. Electrician
c.	A crack in the wall	iii. Carpenters
d.	A fused tube light	iv. Plumber

(A) a-iii, b-iv, c-ii, iv-i
(B) a-iv, b-i, c- iii, iv-ii
(C) a- ii, b-iii, c-i, iv-iv
(D) a-iv, b-iii, c-i, iv-ii

HOTS (ACHIEVERS SECTION)

31. The three different kinds of fabrics are following. Choose the option which shows the correct match.
   (i)   Silk dress
   (ii) Woolen socks
   (iii) Leather shoes
   I.   In what ways are they similar?
   II. Which of them is/are manufactured from animal skin?

	I	II
(A)	They are made of things which were never alive	iii.
(B)	They are made of things which were once alive	iii.
(C)	They are made of things from the ground	ii.
(D)	They are living things	i.

32. Lissy prepared four similar containers, P, Q, R and S. She placed the same amount of cotton wool and five bean seeds in each container but placed them at different places in conditions as shown in the table below.

Container	Air	Water	Sunlight	Place of Container
P	Yes	Yes	Yes	open area
Q	No	Yes	Yes	air-tight container placed next to a window
R	Yes	No	No	the kitchen table
S	Yes	No	No	the freezer

Based on the above data, which container would have seedling after a week?
(A) P only
(B) P and R only
(C) Q and R only
(D) P, R and S only

33. The names of some professionals are hidden in the given word grid.

S	B	G	E	D	P
R	A	R	D	T	N
Q	M	O	I	F	U
D	O	C	T	O	R
W	N	E	O	I	S
O	L	R	R	M	E

I. How many professionals of them belong to same profession?

II. How many of them have the less educational qualification for their occupation?

	I	**II**
(A)	Two	Two
(B)	Two	Three
(C)	One	Three
(D)	Two	One

34. Ananya's daughter, Arti is the niece of Shanu. Rohit is Shanu's son.

Based on the above relationship, select the correct option.

(A) Ananya is sister of Shanu

(B) Rohit is cousin brother of Arti

(C) Ananya and Rohit are not relatives

(D) Both (A) and (B)

35. Rita has gone to Antarctica on a science trip. Select the option which on unscrambling gives name of a clothing that she can wear over there.

(A) TORHSS

(B) KRSIT

(C) ERSEAWT

(D) TOACAIRN

TRANSPORT AND COMMUNICATION

LEARNING OBJECTIVES

➤ Different means of transport: land, water, air transport
➤ Differentiating among computer, mobile, newspaper, T.V.

MULTIPLE CHOICE QUESTIONS

1. The Bharat-Tibet road connects our country to __________.
   (A) Japan
   (B) China
   (C) America
   (D) Pakistan

2. The first railway track in India was laid in __________.
   (A) 1753
   (B) 1853
   (C) 1953
   (D) 1854

3. A lake of salt water separated from the sea is called a/an __________.
   (A) Stream
   (B) Oasis
   (C) Lagoon
   (D) Osmosis

4. The international air service operated by the Indian government is __________.
   (A) Indian Airlines
   (B) Alliance
   (C) Air India
   (D) Sahara Airlines

5. Airplane was invented by __________.
   (A) Thomas Alva Edision
   (B) Alexander Fleming
   (C) The Wright brothers
   (D) The airplane brothers

6. Which of the following helps us to send and receive instant messages?
   (A) Radio
   (B) Television
   (C) Pager
   (D) Postal letter

7. Which of the following is also called cellular phone?
   (A) Hand phones
   (B) Mobile phones
   (C) Telephones
   (D) Wireless phones

8. When telephones are connected across the countries, the call made is said to be __________.
   (A) A local call
   (B) An ISD call
   (C) An STD call
   (D) A mobile call

9. Telephones are connected within the countries by __________.
   (A) Local calls
   (B) ISD calls
   (C) STD calls
   (D) Mobile calls

10. The terms FM and AM are used in regards to __________.
    (A) Movies
    (B) Television
    (C) Radio
    (D) Newspapers

11. Which of the following vehicles is specially designed for physically-challenged persons?

(A) 
(B) 
(C) 
(D) 

12. Look at the grid carefully. How many means of communication are hidden in the grid?

INTERNETOK
LPOSTOFFICE
RTELEVISION
NTELEGRAMPI
KTELEPHONER
INEWSPAPERN

(A) 4　　　　　(B) 6
(C) 7　　　　　(D) 8

13. Which among these is the fastest way to send written message and photographs?
(A) Fax　　　　　(B) E-mail
(C) Post card　　(D) Telegram

14. STD means __________.
(A) Subscriber Trial Dialer
(B) Subscriber Trunk Dialer
(C) Subscriber Transmitted Dialer
(D) Subscriber Trial Date

15. ISD means __________.
(A) International Subscriber Dialing
(B) International Super Dialing
(C) Indian Subscriber Dialing
(D) International Subscriber Dating

16. Select the correct option regarding the following transport vehicle.

(A) It is a tramcar
(B) It is a wheeled vehicle that runs on rails
(C) It is propelled by electricity
(D) All of these

17. This is used for communication by the people working in police and army __________.
(A) Landlines
(B) Newspaper
(C) Wireless communication
(D) Television

18. Sound and pictures both can be broadcast through __________.
(A) Radio　　　　　(B) Fax
(C) Newspapers　　(D) Television

19. This carries letters and parcels from the post office to different places in the city __________.
(A) Postal plane
(B) Postal van
(C) Postal engine
(D) Postal ship

20. Which of the following are means of mass communication?
(i) Newspaper　　　(ii) Internet
(iii) Radio　　　　　(iv) Television
(v) Postcard　　　　(vi) Telephone
(A) (i), (ii), (iii) and (iv)
(B) (ii), (iii), (iv) and (vi)

(C) (v) and (vi)
(D) (iv), (v) and (vi)

21. Steam engine has been replaced by __________.
    (A) Diesel and petrol
    (B) Electric machines
    (C) Mechanical machines
    (D) Mechanical motors

22. New advancements made in the modes of transport and communication are due to the advancement in __________.
    (A) Machinery
    (B) Technology
    (C) Both (A) and (B)
    (D) None of these

23. CNG means __________.
    (A) Compressed Natural Gas
    (B) Composed Natural Gas
    (C) Compressed Nature of Gas
    (D) Compressed Night Gas

24. Newspapers, books and magazine are also called __________.
    (A) Print media
    (B) Electronic media
    (C) Basic means of communication
    (D) Both (A) and (C)

25. CATV means __________.
    (A) Community Antenna Television
    (B) Commercial Antenna Television
    (C) Community Antenna Telescope
    (D) Community Antenna Television

26. An urgent message is sent through a/an __________.
    (A) Inland letter   (B) Telegram
    (C) Postcard   (D) Telephone

27. The instrument that enables us to send messages orally is __________.
    (A) Computer
    (B) Mobile
    (C) Telephone
    (D) Both (B) and (C)

28. The latest mode of communication is/ are __________.
    (A) Computer
    (B) Radio
    (C) Mobile phone
    (D) All of these

29. Which of the following is not a mode of mass communication?
    (A) Newspaper
    (B) Television
    (C) Computer
    (D) Radio

30. Which of the following is not a mode of personal communication?
    (A) Telephone
    (B) Teleprinter
    (C) Magazines
    (D) Books

<hr>

HOTS (ACHIEVERS SECTION)

31. Which of the following will be least useful to send an immediate message?
    (A) Post card
    (B) Short message service
    (C) Fax
    (D) E-mail

32. What is correct regarding the given vehicle?

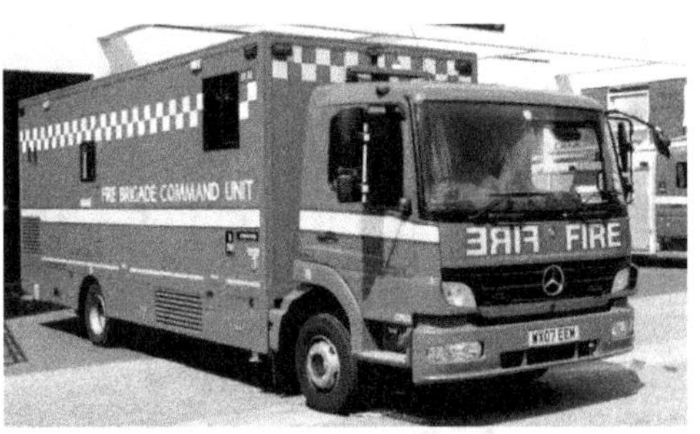

(A) It is special means of transport
(B) It can carry special equipment
(C) It helps to put out fire
(D) It is a public transport

33. The given hand sign represents a _______.
(A) Bird
(B) Fish
(C) Snake
(D) Telephone exchange

34. Select the odd one out among the following.
(A) Radio
(B) Newspaper
(C) Television
(D) Telephone

35. Select the odd one out on the basis of mode of transport.

(A) 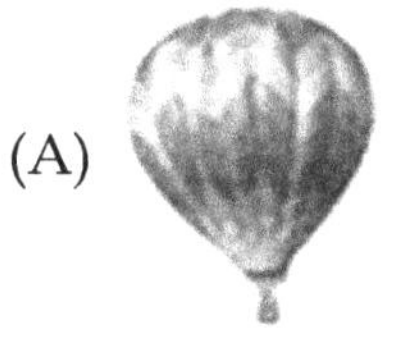

(B) 

(C) 

(D) 

1.	Ⓐ Ⓑ Ⓒ Ⓓ	8.	Ⓐ Ⓑ Ⓒ Ⓓ	15.	Ⓐ Ⓑ Ⓒ Ⓓ	22	Ⓐ Ⓑ Ⓒ Ⓓ	29.	Ⓐ Ⓑ Ⓒ Ⓓ
2.	Ⓐ Ⓑ Ⓒ Ⓓ	9.	Ⓐ Ⓑ Ⓒ Ⓓ	16.	Ⓐ Ⓑ Ⓒ Ⓓ	23.	Ⓐ Ⓑ Ⓒ Ⓓ	30.	Ⓐ Ⓑ Ⓒ Ⓓ
3.	Ⓐ Ⓑ Ⓒ Ⓓ	10.	Ⓐ Ⓑ Ⓒ Ⓓ	17.	Ⓐ Ⓑ Ⓒ Ⓓ	24.	Ⓐ Ⓑ Ⓒ Ⓓ	31.	Ⓐ Ⓑ Ⓒ Ⓓ
4.	Ⓐ Ⓑ Ⓒ Ⓓ	11.	Ⓐ Ⓑ Ⓒ Ⓓ	18.	Ⓐ Ⓑ Ⓒ Ⓓ	25.	Ⓐ Ⓑ Ⓒ Ⓓ	32.	Ⓐ Ⓑ Ⓒ Ⓓ
5.	Ⓐ Ⓑ Ⓒ Ⓓ	12.	Ⓐ Ⓑ Ⓒ Ⓓ	19.	Ⓐ Ⓑ Ⓒ Ⓓ	26.	Ⓐ Ⓑ Ⓒ Ⓓ	33.	Ⓐ Ⓑ Ⓒ Ⓓ
6.	Ⓐ Ⓑ Ⓒ Ⓓ	13.	Ⓐ Ⓑ Ⓒ Ⓓ	20.	Ⓐ Ⓑ Ⓒ Ⓓ	27.	Ⓐ Ⓑ Ⓒ Ⓓ	34.	Ⓐ Ⓑ Ⓒ Ⓓ
7.	Ⓐ Ⓑ Ⓒ Ⓓ	14.	Ⓐ Ⓑ Ⓒ Ⓓ	21.	Ⓐ Ⓑ Ⓒ Ⓓ	28.	Ⓐ Ⓑ Ⓒ Ⓓ	35.	Ⓐ Ⓑ Ⓒ Ⓓ

HUMAN BODY

6

➤ Organs and organ system
➤ Cell organization in human body
➤ Various organ systems of human body

MULTIPLE CHOICE QUESTIONS

1. Number of bones in human skeletal system is _______.
   (A) 206
   (B) 208
   (C) 306
   (D) 308

2. Digestion completes in the _______.
   (A) Stomach
   (B) Small intestine
   (C) Large intestine
   (D) Mouth

3. Heart is an organ of _______.
   (A) Excretory system
   (B) Nervous system
   (C) Digestive system
   (D) Circulatory system

4. Harmful substances are eliminated through the _______.
   (A) Kidney
   (B) Lungs
   (C) Skin
   (D) All of these

5. A group of tissues performing a particular function is called a/an _______.
   (A) Organ System
   (B) Organ
   (C) Cell
   (D) Organism

6. Which of these are circulatory organs?

   (i)  (ii) (iii)

   (A) Both (i) and (ii)
   (B) Both (ii) and (iii)
   (C) Only (i)
   (D) Only (iii)

7. Which organ system in our body is responsible for changing the balloon's shape in the following images?

   (A) Skeletal system
   (B) Circulatory system
   (C) Respiratory system
   (D) Digestive system

8. Look at the following picture carefully. Which of the following organs is/are completely protected inside the following structure?

   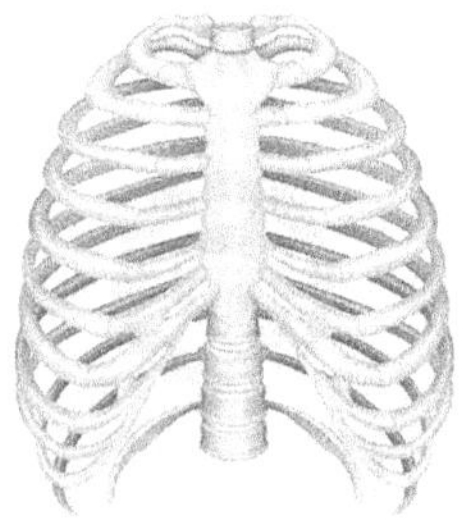

(i)   Heart   (ii) Stomach
(iii) Liver   (iv) Lungs
(A) Both (i) and (ii)
(B) Both (i) and (iv)
(C) Only (ii)
(D) (iii) and (iv)

9. The diagram given below represents an organ which takes in oxygen and gives out carbon dioxide. Name the organ.

Organ ⟵ Oxygen
Organ ⟶ Carbon dioxide

(A) Stomach   (B) Kidney
(C) Lungs   (D) Small intestine

10. Digested food is absorbed by _______.
(A) Blood   (B) Water
(C) Mouth   (D) Heart

11. How many kidneys do we have?
(A) Three   (B) Two
(C) Four   (D) One

12. This organ is located in our chest: _______.
(A) Kidney   (B) Heart
(C) Small intestine (D) Stomach

13. This system gives shape to our body: _______.
(A) Circulatory system
(B) Nervous system
(C) Skeletal system
(D) Muscular system

14. Which organ provides us with the sense of touch and feel?
(A) Skin   (B) Eyes
(C) Nose   (D) Tongue

15. This system helps us eat and process the food that we eat _______.
(A) Reproductive system
(B) Circulatory system
(C) Digestive system
(D) Muscular system

16. The number of muscles present in our body is _______.

(A) 700   (B) 639
(C) 106   (D) 206

17. Pick out the statement which is not true.
(A) Our tongue helps to mix food with saliva in the mouth.
(B) Digestion does not take place in the gullet.
(C) Saliva is a digestive juice.
(D) The digestion of food is completed in the stomach.

18. Digestive juices are produced in the _______.
(i)   Mouth
(ii) Large intestine
(iii) Gullet
(iv) Small intestine
(v)   Stomach
(A) (i), (ii) and (iii)
(B) (iii), (iv) and (v)
(C) (i), (iv) and (v)
(D) (ii) and (v)

19. When Sunil plays basketball, he _______.
(A) Does not make use of any muscles or bones at all.
(B) Uses his muscles and bones to jump and run.
(C) Uses only his bones to run and jump.
(D) Uses only his muscles to move the ball.

20. Our stomach expands when the food enters and contracts when it goes out. Thus the stomach can expand and contract. This is possible because our stomach is made of _______.
(A) Iron   (B) Blood
(C) Muscles   (D) Bones

21. Which of the following is also known as Oesophagos?
(A) Large intestine
(B) Small intestine
(C) Food pipe
(D) Wind pipe

22. Select the incorrect match:
   (A) Excretory system – Remove wastes from the body.
   (B) Respiratory system – Provides oxygen to all parts of the body.
   (C) Nervous system – Controls our action.
   (D) Reproductive system – Helps in producing babies.

23. Which of the following is wrongly classified?

Digestive system	Skeletal system
(A) Stomach	Skull
(B) Mouth	Ribcage
(C) Large intestine	Spine
(D) Nostril	Heart

24. Veins are _______ in colour.
   (A) Red   (B) Purple
   (C) Blue   (D) Green

25. When we touch a hot object, which of the following processes takes place?
   (A) Skin ⟶ Nerves ⟶ hand is pulled back
   (B) Skin ⟶ Nerves ⟶ Brain ⟶ hand is pulled back
   (C) Skin ⟶ Brain ⟶ Nerves ⟶ hand is pulled back
   (D) None of these

HOTS (ACHIEVERS SECTION)

26. See the figure below and choose the correct option.

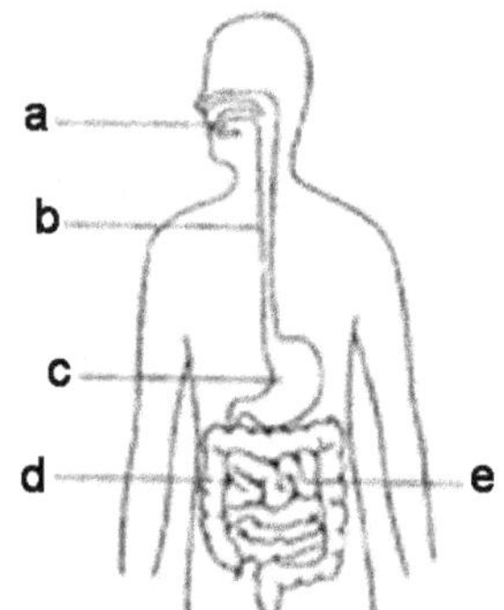

   I. In which part of the digestive system does digestion takes place?
   II. Which is the longest part of the digestive system?

	I	II
(A)	b and d only	a
(B)	a, c and d only	b
(C)	a, c and e only	e
(D)	c, d and e only	c

27. Which of the following options/ statements is correct about the body system shown in the figure below?

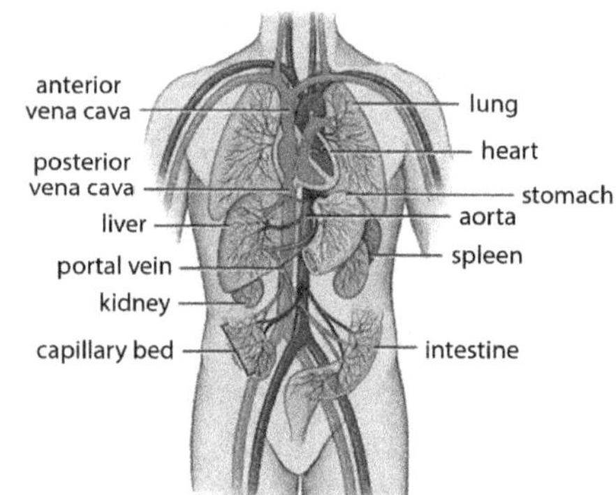

   (A) This system is responsible for body movement.
   (B) This system helps us to get the air we need for survival.
   (C) This system helps us to carry digested food and water to all parts of the body mixed with blood.
   (D) This system helps us to convert the food we eat into a form that can easily be absorbed.

OLYMPIAD WORKBOOK (NSO) CLASS–3

28. The flow diagram given below represents which one of the following system?

Mouth → Food pipe → Stomach → Small intestine → large intestine

(A) Digestive System
(B) Respiratory System
(C) Sensory System
(D) Nervous System

29. The stomach is about 8 inches long and is a sac that is shaped like the letter "j". What is food mixed with when it is in the stomach?

(A) Enzymes   (B) Acids
(C) Saliva   (D) Germs

30. Directions: Using the clues unscramble the letters and find the organ systems. A. Our body gets its shape from __________.

S	L	E	A	L	K	E	T

(A) nervous   (B) circulatory
(C) skeletal   (D) reproductive

1.	Ⓐ Ⓑ Ⓒ Ⓓ	7.	Ⓐ Ⓑ Ⓒ Ⓓ	13.	Ⓐ Ⓑ Ⓒ Ⓓ	19	Ⓐ Ⓑ Ⓒ Ⓓ	25.	Ⓐ Ⓑ Ⓒ Ⓓ
2.	Ⓐ Ⓑ Ⓒ Ⓓ	8.	Ⓐ Ⓑ Ⓒ Ⓓ	14.	Ⓐ Ⓑ Ⓒ Ⓓ	20.	Ⓐ Ⓑ Ⓒ Ⓓ	26.	Ⓐ Ⓑ Ⓒ Ⓓ
3.	Ⓐ Ⓑ Ⓒ Ⓓ	9.	Ⓐ Ⓑ Ⓒ Ⓓ	15.	Ⓐ Ⓑ Ⓒ Ⓓ	21.	Ⓐ Ⓑ Ⓒ Ⓓ	27.	Ⓐ Ⓑ Ⓒ Ⓓ
4.	Ⓐ Ⓑ Ⓒ Ⓓ	10.	Ⓐ Ⓑ Ⓒ Ⓓ	16.	Ⓐ Ⓑ Ⓒ Ⓓ	22.	Ⓐ Ⓑ Ⓒ Ⓓ	28.	Ⓐ Ⓑ Ⓒ Ⓓ
5.	Ⓐ Ⓑ Ⓒ Ⓓ	11.	Ⓐ Ⓑ Ⓒ Ⓓ	17.	Ⓐ Ⓑ Ⓒ Ⓓ	23.	Ⓐ Ⓑ Ⓒ Ⓓ	29.	Ⓐ Ⓑ Ⓒ Ⓓ
6.	Ⓐ Ⓑ Ⓒ Ⓓ	12.	Ⓐ Ⓑ Ⓒ Ⓓ	18.	Ⓐ Ⓑ Ⓒ Ⓓ	24.	Ⓐ Ⓑ Ⓒ Ⓓ	30.	Ⓐ Ⓑ Ⓒ Ⓓ

EARTH AND UNIVERSE

LEARNING OBJECTIVES

➤ The planet Earth
➤ The movement of the Earth
➤ natural satellites
➤ The shape and size of the Earth
➤ The solar system

MULTIPLE CHOICE QUESTIONS

1. One of the planets known to have rings is __________.
   - (A) Venus
   - (B) Saturn
   - (C) Mars
   - (D) Pluto

2. Which of the following is not a Jovian planet (gas giant)?
   - (A) Earth
   - (B) Uranus
   - (C) Neptune
   - (D) Saturn

3. Which of the following is not a terrestrial planet?
   - (A) Mars
   - (B) Earth
   - (C) Jupiter
   - (D) Mercury

4. The formation of the solar system from a huge cloud of dust and gases is called the __________.
   - (A) Protoplanet theory
   - (B) Nebular theory
   - (C) Solar theory
   - (D) Planetesimal theory

5. Which of the following is not considered a part of the solar system?
   - (A) Jovian planets
   - (B) Terrestrial planets
   - (C) Sun
   - (D) Galaxies

6. The Jovian planets contain a large percentage of which of the following gases?
   - (A) Nitrogen and argon
   - (B) Oxygen and nitrogen
   - (C) Hydrogen and helium
   - (D) Hydrogen and oxygen

7. Which planet has a cratered surface similar to the Earth's moon?
   - (A) Venus
   - (B) Saturn
   - (C) Mars
   - (D) Mercury

8. The planet with the greatest temperature extremes is __________.
   - (A) Earth
   - (C) Mars
   - (B) Venus
   - (D) Mercury

9. Which planet has a dense carbon-dioxide atmosphere and high surface temperatures?
   - (A) Venus
   - (B) Earth
   - (C) Mars
   - (D) Mercury

10. The atmosphere of Venus is composed primarily of __________.
    - (A) Water vapour
    - (B) Oxygen
    - (C) Hydrogen
    - (D) Carbon dioxide

11. Which planet has a greater mass than the combined mass of all the remaining planets and their moons?
(A) Venus (B) Saturn
(C) Jupiter (D) Pluto

12. Which of the following is a characteristic of Jupiter?
(A) Huge rotating storms
(B) Dense atmosphere
(C) Thin ring system
(D) All of these

13. The relatively small, rocky bodies generally found orbiting between Mars and Jupiter are known as _________.
(A) Comets (B) Asteroids
(C) Satellites (D) Meteoroids

14. Which regions are comets with short orbital periods located in?
(A) Kuiper belt
(B) Oort cloud
(C) Inner solar system
(D) None of these

15. Which of the following planets scientists do not consider a major planet?
(A) Saturn (B) Pluto
(C) Mercury (D) Neptune

16. Small bodies that orbit planets are called _________.

(A) Comets (B) Planet Simals
(C) Moons (D) Protoplanets

17. When early Earth's atmosphere formed, which of the following gases were lost because Earth's gravity was too weak?
(A) Helium and hydrogen
(B) Helium and nitrogen
(C) Hydrogen and ozone
(D) Oxygen and helium

18. Which of the following planets experiences a runaway greenhouse effect?
(A) Venus (B) Mars
(C) Pluto (D) Earth

19. The right combination of temperature, water and oxygen _________.
(A) Affects neptune's orbit
(B) Supports life on earth
(C) Causes gas giants to form
(D) Results in storms on Jupiter

20. A rotating cloud of gas and dust from which the Earth's solar system formed is called an _________.
(A) Supernova
(B) Astronomical explosion
(C) Solar nebula
(D) Solar eclipse

21. Which of the following statements best describes how the planets of the solar system formed?
(A) They are condensed rings of matter thrown off by the young sun.
(B) They are the remains of an exploded star once paired with the sun.
(C) The sun's gravity caught them from smaller, older nearby stars.
(D) They were formed from a nebular cloud of dust and gas.

22. Which of the following events is NOT caused by only the rotation of the Earth about its own axis?
(A) Sunflowers turning to face the sun in the day.
(B) Cycle of the day and night.
(C) Cycle of the phases of the moon.
(D) The leaves of the rain tree closing every evening.

23. _________ can be sent to other planets to gather information.
(A) Man-made satellites
(B) The moon
(C) The sun
(D) Natural satellites

24. Which of the following statements about the moon is not true?
(A) It is a natural satellite of the Earth.
(B) It is smaller than the Earth.
(C) It can be seen because it gives out light.
(D) It has no air and water.

25. If moon is replaced by the sun, which of the following will happen on Earth?
    (i) Lightning and thunder storms
    (ii) Boiling hot atmosphere
    (iii) Rain
    (iv) Freezing cold atmosphere
    (A) (i) only
    (B) (i) and (ii) only
    (C) (iii) Only
    (D) (i), (ii) and (iii)

26. I am the brightest and the hottest member of the solar system I revolve around the Sun. Who am I?
    (A) Evening star
    (B) Blue planet
    (C) Red planet
    (D) North star

27. Select the incorrect statement regarding the rotation of the Earth.
    (A) The Earth completes one rotation in 24 hours.
    (B) The Earth rotates from West to East.
    (C) The rotation of the Earth causes changes of season.
    (D) The rotation of the Earth causes day and night.

28. Why is the sun important to the Earth?
    (i) It rotates around the Earth to give us seasons.
    (ii) It provides heat to enable living things to survive on Earth.
    (iii) It provides green plants with light energy to make food.
    (A) (i) and (ii) only
    (B) (ii) and (iii) only
    (C) (iii) only
    (D) (i) and (iii) only

29. The imaginary line dividing the Earth into two halves is called __________.
    (A) The orbit
    (B) The equator
    (C) The half time
    (D) The path

30. The Earth completes one rotation in __________.
    (A) One hour
    (B) One day
    (C) One week
    (D) One year

<hr>

HOTS (ACHIEVERS SECTION)

31. Look at the following diagram and choose the correct option.

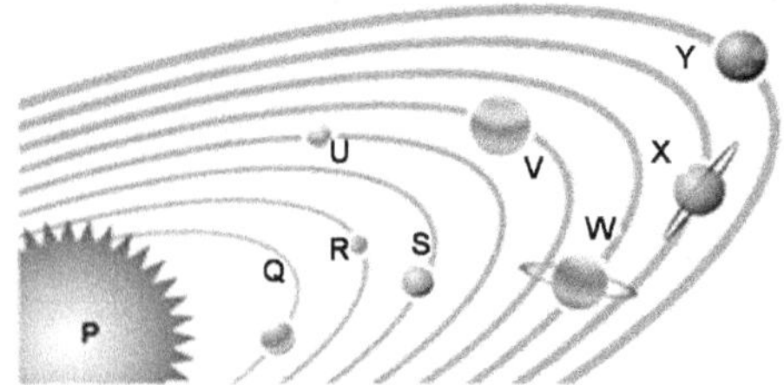

    I. Which letter in the solar system diagram above shows Mars?
    II. Which object the letter 'P' shows in the diagram?

	I	II
(A)	Q	Star
(B)	R	Planet
(C)	U	Star
(D)	V	Comet

32. A group of stars forming a pattern is shown below. Such kind of groups are called:

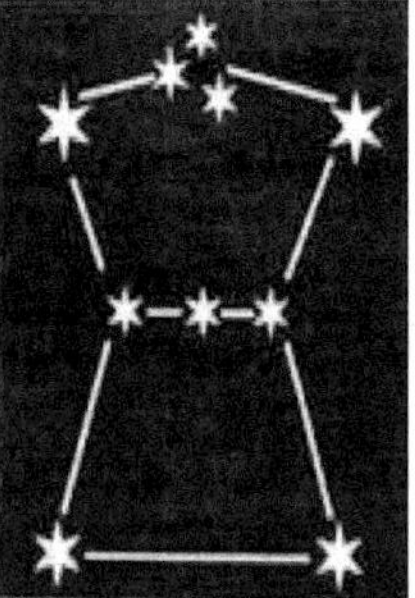

    (A) stars
    (B) planets
    (C) constellations
    (D) groups

33. This diagram of Earth represents:

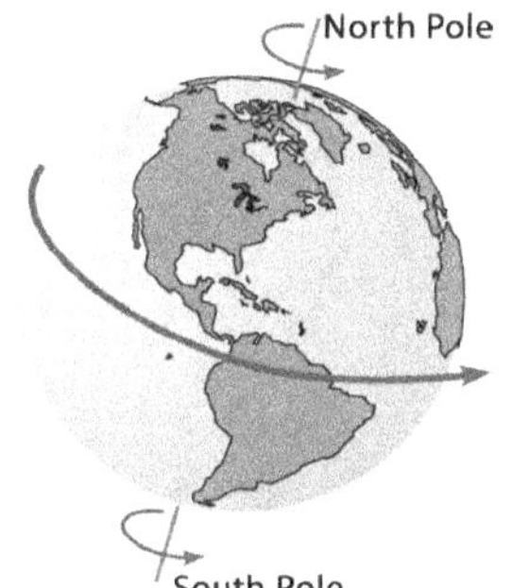

(A) rotation
(B) revolution
(C) formation of days and nights
(D) formation of planets

34. Which of these shapes does the Moon never take?

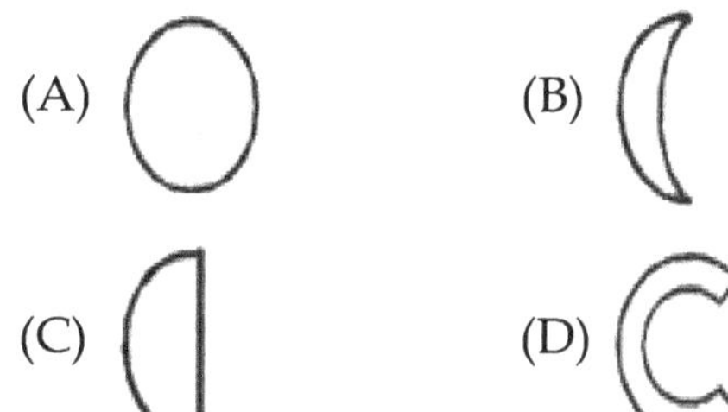

35. When we observe a ship sailing away from the shore the tower part of the ship disappears first from the sight. Then at last, the flag at the top pole disappears. This is possible only if the Earth is:

(A) round shaped
(B) zig zag shaped
(C) slate shaped
(D) flat

1.	Ⓐ Ⓑ Ⓒ Ⓓ	8.	Ⓐ Ⓑ Ⓒ Ⓓ	15.	Ⓐ Ⓑ Ⓒ Ⓓ	22	Ⓐ Ⓑ Ⓒ Ⓓ	29.	Ⓐ Ⓑ Ⓒ Ⓓ
2.	Ⓐ Ⓑ Ⓒ Ⓓ	9.	Ⓐ Ⓑ Ⓒ Ⓓ	16.	Ⓐ Ⓑ Ⓒ Ⓓ	23.	Ⓐ Ⓑ Ⓒ Ⓓ	30.	Ⓐ Ⓑ Ⓒ Ⓓ
3.	Ⓐ Ⓑ Ⓒ Ⓓ	10.	Ⓐ Ⓑ Ⓒ Ⓓ	17.	Ⓐ Ⓑ Ⓒ Ⓓ	24.	Ⓐ Ⓑ Ⓒ Ⓓ	31.	Ⓐ Ⓑ Ⓒ Ⓓ
4.	Ⓐ Ⓑ Ⓒ Ⓓ	11.	Ⓐ Ⓑ Ⓒ Ⓓ	18.	Ⓐ Ⓑ Ⓒ Ⓓ	25.	Ⓐ Ⓑ Ⓒ Ⓓ	32.	Ⓐ Ⓑ Ⓒ Ⓓ
5.	Ⓐ Ⓑ Ⓒ Ⓓ	12.	Ⓐ Ⓑ Ⓒ Ⓓ	19.	Ⓐ Ⓑ Ⓒ Ⓓ	26.	Ⓐ Ⓑ Ⓒ Ⓓ	33.	Ⓐ Ⓑ Ⓒ Ⓓ
6.	Ⓐ Ⓑ Ⓒ Ⓓ	13.	Ⓐ Ⓑ Ⓒ Ⓓ	20.	Ⓐ Ⓑ Ⓒ Ⓓ	27.	Ⓐ Ⓑ Ⓒ Ⓓ	34.	Ⓐ Ⓑ Ⓒ Ⓓ
7.	Ⓐ Ⓑ Ⓒ Ⓓ	14.	Ⓐ Ⓑ Ⓒ Ⓓ	21.	Ⓐ Ⓑ Ⓒ Ⓓ	28.	Ⓐ Ⓑ Ⓒ Ⓓ	35.	Ⓐ Ⓑ Ⓒ Ⓓ

MATTER AND MATERIALS

LEARNING OBJECTIVES

➤ Matter
➤ Different forms of matter

MULTIPLE CHOICE QUESTIONS

1. The amount of space an object takes up is called ___________.
   (A) Mass (B) Matter
   (C) Volume (D) Property

2. The state of matter of rocks is ___________.
   (A) Liquid
   (B) Gaseous
   (C) Solid
   (D) Both (A) and (B)

3. When describing the colour, size, shape, or smell of an object, you are describing the:
   (A) Properties of matter
   (B) States of matter
   (C) Volume of matter
   (D) Mass of matter

4. Mass is ___________.
   (A) The measure of how much material an object is made of
   (B) Anything that takes up space
   (C) The color or shape of an object
   (D) Both (B) and (C)

5. The conversion of matter from solid state to liquid state is called ___________.
   (A) Vaporization
   (B) Melting
   (C) Evaporation
   (D) Condensation

6. Which of the following does not take the shape of the container it is in?
   (A) A pencil (B) Oil
   (C) Water (D) Air

7. Which state of matter spreads itself thinner and thinner until it fills the entire volume of the container irrespective of its size?
   (A) Liquid
   (B) Gas
   (C) Solid
   (D) Both (A) and (B)

8. Choose the correct statement:
   (i) In solids the molecules are packed together closely.
   (ii) In gases the molecules are spread out the most.
   (iii) In liquids the molecules are packed close together, but not as tightly as solids.
   (A) Statement (i) alone is right
   (B) Statement (ii) alone is right
   (C) Statement (iii) alone is right
   (D) All of these

9. Pick the true statement(s):
   (A) An ice cube becomes gas at its melting point
   (B) Gases can freeze
   (C) An ice cube becomes liquid at its melting point
   (D) Both (B) and (C)

10. Matter has __________.
    (A) No mass but occupies space
    (B) Mass but occupies no space
    (C) Mass and occupies space
    (D) No mass and occupies no space

11. The gaseous form of water is called __________.
    (A) Water gas
    (B) Water vapour
    (C) Fog
    (D) Snow

12. The state of matter with only one free surface is __________.
    (A) Liquid
    (B) Gas
    (C) Solid
    (D) Plasma

13. Which of the following is made of only one material?
    (A) Pen
    (B) Sweater
    (C) Newspaper
    (D) Both (B) and (C)

14. Look at the following object carefully. This object is __________.

    (i)   Soft
    (ii) Paper-based product
    (iii) Not water proof
    (iv) Non-flexible
    (A) (i) only
    (B) (i) and (iii)
    (C) (ii), (iii) and (iv)
    (D) (i) and (iv)

15. A property not possessed by a fluid __________.
    (A) It can flow
    (B) It has mass
    (C) It has a definite shape
    (D) Can be perceived by our senses

16. Which of these is a characteristic property of gases?
    (A) Gases are not rigid at all
    (B) Gases are not compressible
    (C) Gases have particles in fixed positions
    (D) Gases have high density

17. A solid has __________.
    (A) Maximum intermolecular space
    (B) Definite mass but no definite volume
    (C) Very high compressibility
    (D) Maximum intermolecular force of attraction

18. The conversion of a gas into liquid is called __________.
    (A) Condensation
    (B) Sublimation
    (C) Vapourisation
    (D) Solidification

19. The process by which wet clothes dry up is called __________.
    (A) Evaporation
    (B) Condensation
    (C) Boiling
    (D) Solidification

20. Matter changes from one state to another with change in __________.

(A) Density

(B) Temperature

(C) Volume

(D) Height

21. The freezing point of pure water is __________.

(A) 100°C

(B) 0°C

(C) 5°C

(D) 78.3°C

22. The force between particles of matter is called __________.

(A) Cohesive force

(B) Adhesive force

(C) Kinetic energy

(D) Thermal energy

23. Which of the following undergoes sublimation?

(A) Phenyl

(B) Petrol

(C) Diesel

(D) Naphthalene balls

24. Look at the given picture. What is the person trying to test about plastic tube?

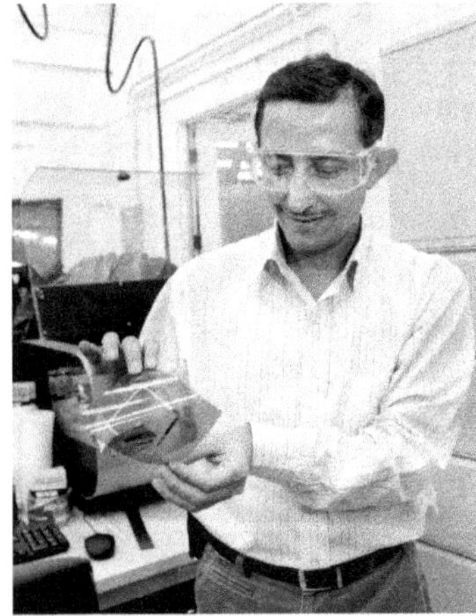

(A) Its flexibility

(B) Its hardness

(C) Its strength

(D) Its ability to float or sink in water

25. Look at the given picture carefully. It is made of gold and gold is a/an __________.

(A) Atom

(B) Mixture

(C) Element

(D) Compound

26. Sugar dissolved in water is a/an __________.

(A) Atom

(B) Mixture

(C) Element

(D) Sloution

27. Look at the following picture carefully. The contents of this container can be classified as __________.

(A) Atom

(B) Mixture

(C) Element

(D) Compound

28. What is an element?
    (A) A pure substance
    (B) Matter of one type of atom
    (C) Can be broken down
    (D) Both (A) and (C)

29. Which is not an example of a chemical change?
    (A) Rust
    (B) Pollution
    (C) Melting
    (D) Toasted marshmallows

30. Which is not an example of a physical change?
    (A) Cutting
    (B) Toasted marshmallow
    (C) Freezing
    (D) Melting

HOTS (ACHIEVERS SECTION)

31. The flow chart below shows the characteristics of a few substances. Choose the corret option based on given chart.

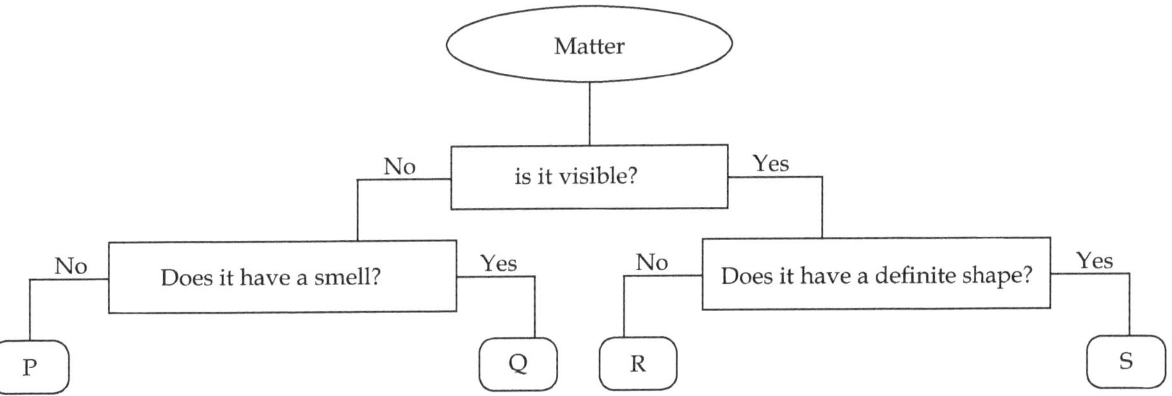

    (A) R - Sugar solution, S - Hydrogen gas
    (B) Q - Ice, R - Cooking gas
    (C) P - Rubber, R - Ice cream
    (D) Q - Cooking gas, S - Plastic bottle

32. Ravi and Shashi were standing as shown here. Ravi waved to Shashi and she smiled in reply. Sheet X in between them can be made of

    (A) Wood   (B) Iron
    (C) Rubber   (D) Glass

33. Select the product which is made of only one material.

    (A) 

    (B) 

    (C) 

    (D) Both (A) and (C)

34. Rahul took a container of 1500 cm^3 volume and pumped 500 cm^3 air into it. Now, the volume of air in the container is _______.

(A) 1500 cm^3
(B) 500 cm^3
(C) 2000 cm^3
(D) Cannot say

35. Refer to the given diagram and select the correct option regarding it.

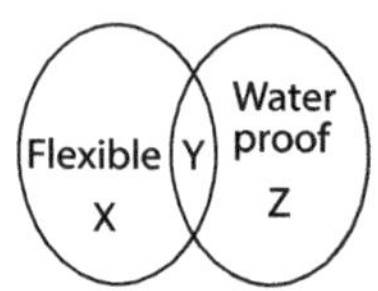

(A) X - Rubber, Y - Plastic
(B) Z - Wood, X - Cardboard
(C) Y - Sponge, X - Rubber
(D) Z - Glass, X - Paper

1.	Ⓐ Ⓑ Ⓒ Ⓓ	8.	Ⓐ Ⓑ Ⓒ Ⓓ	15.	Ⓐ Ⓑ Ⓒ Ⓓ	22	Ⓐ Ⓑ Ⓒ Ⓓ	29.	Ⓐ Ⓑ Ⓒ Ⓓ
2.	Ⓐ Ⓑ Ⓒ Ⓓ	9.	Ⓐ Ⓑ Ⓒ Ⓓ	16.	Ⓐ Ⓑ Ⓒ Ⓓ	23.	Ⓐ Ⓑ Ⓒ Ⓓ	30.	Ⓐ Ⓑ Ⓒ Ⓓ
3.	Ⓐ Ⓑ Ⓒ Ⓓ	10.	Ⓐ Ⓑ Ⓒ Ⓓ	17.	Ⓐ Ⓑ Ⓒ Ⓓ	24.	Ⓐ Ⓑ Ⓒ Ⓓ	31.	Ⓐ Ⓑ Ⓒ Ⓓ
4.	Ⓐ Ⓑ Ⓒ Ⓓ	11.	Ⓐ Ⓑ Ⓒ Ⓓ	18.	Ⓐ Ⓑ Ⓒ Ⓓ	25.	Ⓐ Ⓑ Ⓒ Ⓓ	32.	Ⓐ Ⓑ Ⓒ Ⓓ
5.	Ⓐ Ⓑ Ⓒ Ⓓ	12.	Ⓐ Ⓑ Ⓒ Ⓓ	19.	Ⓐ Ⓑ Ⓒ Ⓓ	26.	Ⓐ Ⓑ Ⓒ Ⓓ	33.	Ⓐ Ⓑ Ⓒ Ⓓ
6.	Ⓐ Ⓑ Ⓒ Ⓓ	13.	Ⓐ Ⓑ Ⓒ Ⓓ	20.	Ⓐ Ⓑ Ⓒ Ⓓ	27.	Ⓐ Ⓑ Ⓒ Ⓓ	34.	Ⓐ Ⓑ Ⓒ Ⓓ
7.	Ⓐ Ⓑ Ⓒ Ⓓ	14.	Ⓐ Ⓑ Ⓒ Ⓓ	21.	Ⓐ Ⓑ Ⓒ Ⓓ	28.	Ⓐ Ⓑ Ⓒ Ⓓ	35.	Ⓐ Ⓑ Ⓒ Ⓓ

OLYMPIAD WORKBOOK (NSO) CLASS—3

LIGHT, FORCE AND SOUND

LEARNING OBJECTIVES

➤ Light and its sources
➤ Force and its different types
➤ The concept of sound

➤ Light and shadow
➤ Push and pull movements

MULTIPLE CHOICE QUESTIONS

1. What is light?
   (A) What we see with our eyes.
   (B) A form of energy that travels in waves.
   (C) A form of work that reflects.
   (D) A form of force that reflects.

2. In order for a shadow to occur, which of the following is not necessary?
   (A) Light source
   (B) Surface
   (C) Object
   (D) The sun

3. Which of the following variables does not affect the shadow of an object?
   (A) Distance from the sun
   (B) Angle of the sun's rays hitting the object
   (C) Size of the sun
   (D) Size of the object

4. Which of the following does not have its own light?
   (A) The Moon   (B) The Sun
   (C) Mars   (D) Jupiter

5. We can see any object only when there is _______.

   (A) Darkness
   (B) A cloud
   (C) Light
   (D) Night

6. Sound travels through _______.
   (A) Sky   (B) Space
   (C) Air   (D) Vaccum

7. When you pull a toy car, you need to apply _______.
   (A) Work   (B) Force
   (C) Light   (D) Sound

8. Which of the following are luminous?
   (A) Campfire
   (B) The moon
   (C) A hot toaster filament
   (D) Both (A) and (B)

9. Trees provide shade to us when they _______.
   (A) Bounce light
   (B) Need water
   (C) Are under a cloud
   (D) Block sunlight

10. Which of these will most likely form a dark shadow on a sunny day?

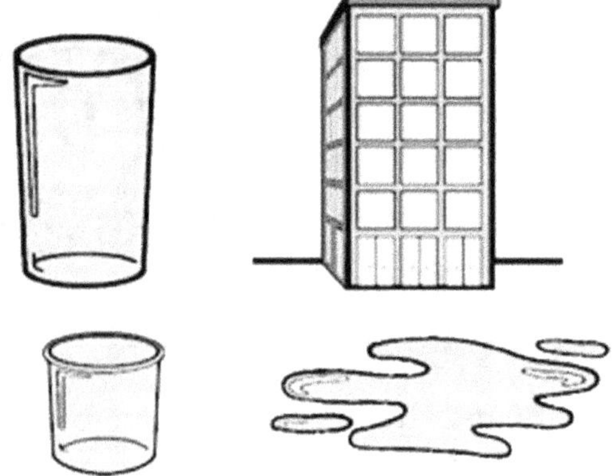

(A) Clear glass
(B) A building
(C) Clear cup
(D) Water

11. Which one of the following object makes no sound when it is dropped from a height?
(A) Coin
(B) Basketball
(C) Glass beaker
(D) Feather

12. The strings on a guitar make noise because they __________.
(A) Stretch
(B) Break
(C) Vibrate
(D) Stay still

13. A teacher placed a stick in the middle of a field. Four students were asked to observe the shadow of the stick and to state their observation. Which student is correct?

Rohan: A shadow is a living thing as it can move and grow in length.

Shobhit: A shadow is a non-living thing as it cannot reproduce and it is dependent on movement of the Earth.

Renu: A shadow is a living thing as it responds to the positions of the sun in the sky.

Sonali: A shadow is a non-living thing and its position and length depend on the sun's position.
(A) Rohan only
(B) Sonali and Shobhit
(C) Renu only
(D) Renu and Sonali

14. Which series of numbers shows the pictures from coldest to hottest?

(A) II, III, I   (B) I, III, II
(C) I, II, III   (D) III, I, II

15. Ananya is pushing a box. On which surface is it easier to move the box?
(A) Hot surface
(B) Wet surface
(C) Rough surface
(D) Dry surface

16. There is a banana peel on the ground. What might happen to the person who steps on it?
(A) The person might fall because the banana peel will reduce gravity.
(B) The person might not fall because the banana peel will not reduce gravity.
(C) The person might fall because the banana peel will reduce the friction between his shoe and the ground.
(D) The person might fall because the banana peel will increase friction between his shoe and the ground.

17. We can see a tree in the daytime, because __________.
(A) Light travels from our eyes to the tree.
(B) The tree reflects sunlight into our eyes.
(C) The tree allows light to pass through it.
(D) The tree gives off light of its own.

18. Sunil was playing with a ball. He picked up the ball to a certain height and let it fall. He observed that the ball dropped to the ground. Choose the correct option.
R: What force caused the ball to drop to the ground?
S: Is the force a push or pull?

	R	S
(A)	Gravity	Push
(B)	Friction	Push
(C)	Friction	Pull
(D)	Gravity	Pull

19. What is the human audible range?
    (A) 10–35,000 Hz
    (B) 20–20,000 Hz
    (C) 50–50,000 Hz
    (D) 5,000–10,000 Hz

20. What is the infrasonic range of sound?
    (A) Sounds above 50 Hz
    (B) Sounds below 50 Hz
    (C) Sounds above 500 Hz
    (D) Sounds below 20 Hz

21. This term is not related to sound ______.
    (A) Frequency   (B) Vibration
    (C) Hertz   (D) Celsius

22. The unit of frequency is ______.
    (A) Gram   (B) Centimeter
    (C) Hertz   (D) Celsius

23. Which one of the following is the loudest?
    (A) Sparrow   (B) Lion
    (C) Monkey   (D) Deer

24. The motion of an object sliding on a floor is a ______.
    (A) Transitory motion
    (B) Transaction motion
    (C) Translatory motion
    (D) Both (B) and (C)

25. Movement in a circular path is an example of __________.
    (A) Rotatory motion
    (B) Translatory force
    (C) Rotational motion
    (D) Rotatory force

HOTS (ACHIEVERS SECTION)

26. Match the objects with their names and choose the correct option.

	I	II	III
i.		Stairs	inclined plane
ii.		Doorknob	inclined plane
iii.		Broom	lever

    (A) iii only   (B) i and iii only
    (C) i only   (D) ii and iii only

27. Select the correct option based on the given questions.
    I. Which of the following is not true about a force?
    II. Describe motion in brief?

	I	II
(A)	It sets an object into motion	The push or pull of an object.
(B)	It stops a moving object	When an object changes position.
(C)	Force cannot be applied on static objects	A force that works against motion.
(D)	It is a push or a pull	When an object changes position with respect to time.

28. Select the odd one out.

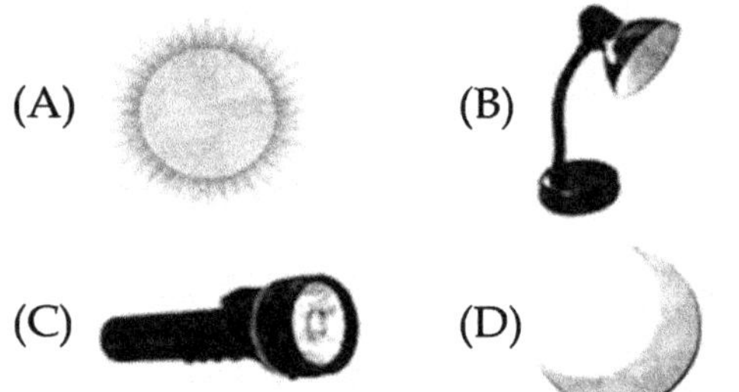

(A)   (B)

(C)   (D)

29. Ritu cannot hear what Megha is saying, X must be _______.

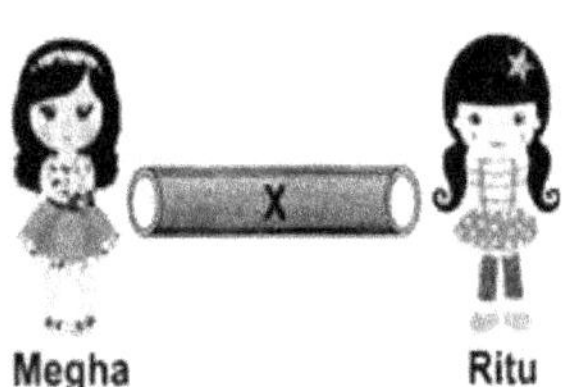

(A) Solid
(B) Liquid
(C) Gas
(D) Vacuum

30. Sahil shone a torch and blew a horn at the same time, while standing at 15 m distance from Amit. Amit will _______.

(A) First hear the sound then see the light
(B) First see the light then hear the sound
(C) See the light and hear the sound at the same time
(D) None of these

1.	Ⓐ Ⓑ Ⓒ Ⓓ	7.	Ⓐ Ⓑ Ⓒ Ⓓ	13.	Ⓐ Ⓑ Ⓒ Ⓓ	19	Ⓐ Ⓑ Ⓒ Ⓓ	25.	Ⓐ Ⓑ Ⓒ Ⓓ
2.	Ⓐ Ⓑ Ⓒ Ⓓ	8.	Ⓐ Ⓑ Ⓒ Ⓓ	14.	Ⓐ Ⓑ Ⓒ Ⓓ	20.	Ⓐ Ⓑ Ⓒ Ⓓ	26.	Ⓐ Ⓑ Ⓒ Ⓓ
3.	Ⓐ Ⓑ Ⓒ Ⓓ	9.	Ⓐ Ⓑ Ⓒ Ⓓ	15.	Ⓐ Ⓑ Ⓒ Ⓓ	21.	Ⓐ Ⓑ Ⓒ Ⓓ	27.	Ⓐ Ⓑ Ⓒ Ⓓ
4.	Ⓐ Ⓑ Ⓒ Ⓓ	10.	Ⓐ Ⓑ Ⓒ Ⓓ	16.	Ⓐ Ⓑ Ⓒ Ⓓ	22.	Ⓐ Ⓑ Ⓒ Ⓓ	28.	Ⓐ Ⓑ Ⓒ Ⓓ
5.	Ⓐ Ⓑ Ⓒ Ⓓ	11.	Ⓐ Ⓑ Ⓒ Ⓓ	17.	Ⓐ Ⓑ Ⓒ Ⓓ	23.	Ⓐ Ⓑ Ⓒ Ⓓ	29.	Ⓐ Ⓑ Ⓒ Ⓓ
6.	Ⓐ Ⓑ Ⓒ Ⓓ	12.	Ⓐ Ⓑ Ⓒ Ⓓ	18.	Ⓐ Ⓑ Ⓒ Ⓓ	24.	Ⓐ Ⓑ Ⓒ Ⓓ	30.	Ⓐ Ⓑ Ⓒ Ⓓ

OUR ENVIRONMENT 

LEARNING OBJECTIVES

➤ Components of Environment
➤ Types of Soil
➤ Pollution and pollutants

MULTIPLE CHOICE QUESTIONS

1. Which of the following is not true for the care of teeth?
   (A) We should not chew the food
   (B) We should not eat too many sweets
   (C) We should brush twice a day
   (D) We should eat raw fruits and vegetables

2. Mosquitoes spread:
   (A) cancer
   (B) stomach ache
   (C) malaria
   (D) blood pressure

3. Stagnant water breeds:
   (A) mosquitoes
   (B) frogs
   (C) fishes
   (D) animals

4. What should be sprayed on stagnated water to prevent mosquitoes breeding?
   (A) Water
   (B) Boiled water done clear
   (C) ORS
   (D) Kerosene

5. Which of the following is the correct way to dispose garbage?
   (A) Throwing it on the road
   (B) Throwing it into covered pita
   (C) Leaving it where it is
   (D) Burning it on the roads

6. Noise is produced from these sources
   (A) fire crackers
   (B) vehicles
   (C) loud music
   (D) all of these

7. Noise pollution can cause
   (A) loss of hearing
   (B) cold & cough
   (C) none of these
   (D) breathing problem

8. Harmful substances when dumped in the soil.
   (A) air pollution
   (B) soil pollution
   (C) water pollution
   (D) noise pollution

9. Farmers use pesticides to save crops from
   (A) humans
   (B) doctors
   (C) insects
   (D) friends

10. We must keep our surroundings
    (A) neat & clean
    (B) wet
    (C) dirty
    (D) none of these

11. Which one is a bad habit?
    (A) chewing tobacco
    (B) smoking
    (C) spitting on roads
    (D) all of these

12. How can we help the environment
    (A) reusing waste
    (B) reducing waste
    (C) recycling waste
    (D) all of these

13. Waste water and human excreta is called
    (A) sewage   (B) scrap
    (C) yield   (D) none of these
14. Loud speakers and honking of vehicles causes
    (A) soil pollution   (B) water pollution
    (C) air pollution   (D) noise pollution
15. __________ is a harmful gas which causes air pollution
    (A) nitrogen   (B) carbondioxide
    (C) oxygen   (D) none of these
16. Pollution is the process of making the environment
    (A) dirty   (B) happy
    (C) clean   (D) All of above

17. The substance which pollutes the environment is called the
    (A) environment   (B) pollutant
    (C) air   (D) None
18. The types of pollutions are
    (A) water pollution   (B) air pollution
    (C) noise pollution   (D) all of these
19. The Earth's atmosphere is made up of these gases
    (A) nitrogen   (B) oxygen
    (C) carbon dioxide   (D) all of these
20. Air pollution causes due to
    (A) smoke   (B) fire crackers
    (C) both   (D) none of these

HOTS (ACHIEVERS SECTION)

21. Trees release the gas __________.
    (A) oxygen   (B) carbondioxide
    (C) helium   (D) nitrogen
22. Air pollution causes __________.
    (A) happiness   (B) global warming
    (C) population   (D) cold
23. When harmful substances are releases into the water bodies it is called __________.

    (A) noise pollution   (B) air pollution
    (C) soil pollution   (D) water pollution
24. We need water for doing __________.
    (A) bathing   (B) cooking
    (C) drinking   (D) all of these
25. Whenever we hear very loud noise it cause __________.
    (A) irritation   (B) comfort
    (C) happiness   (D) all of these

—Darken Your Choice with HB Pencil—

1.	A B C D	6.	A B C D	11.	A B C D	16	A B C D	21.	A B C D
2.	A B C D	7.	A B C D	12.	A B C D	17.	A B C D	22.	A B C D
3.	A B C D	8.	A B C D	13.	A B C D	18.	A B C D	23.	A B C D
4.	A B C D	9.	A B C D	14.	A B C D	19.	A B C D	23.	A B C D
5.	A B C D	10.	A B C D	15.	A B C D	20.	A B C D	25.	A B C D

LOGICAL REASONING 

LEARNING OBJECTIVES

- ➤ Finding out the next shape in a series
- ➤ Identifying a relationship between words, events, objects
- ➤ The concept of series completion
- ➤ The types of classification
- ➤ Various types of coding and decoding
- ➤ Solving ranking based problems
- ➤ Mirror images and water images
- ➤ Concept of figure matrix
- ➤ Congruent figures
- ➤ Solving problems by using the given tips

MULTIPLE CHOICE QUESTIONS

1. What are the next two shapes?

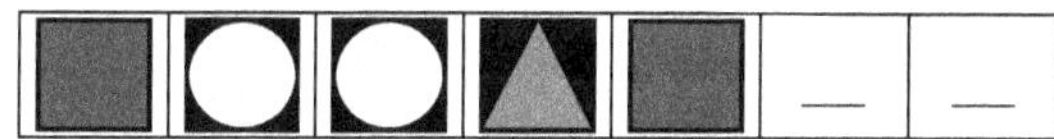

(A) Circle, circle
(B) Triangle, circle
(C) Circle, triangle
(D) Square, circle

2. What are the next two shapes?

(A) Circle, circle
(B) Triangle, square
(C) Circle, triangle
(D) Square, circle

3. See the number pattern in star A. The first point has a value of 3. Then look a star B. Use the same number pattern to find out the value of the other points.

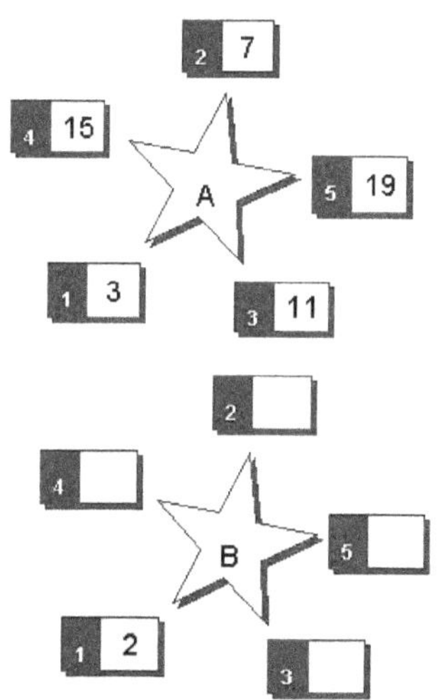

(A) 5, 7, 9, 18
(B) 4, 6, 8, 10
(C) 6, 10, 14, 18
(D) 10, 12, 14, 16

4. What number should be on the other points if you follow the same pattern?

2 6
4 12
A 5 15
1 3
3 9

2
4 B 5
1 5
3

(A) 10, 15, 20, 25　　(B) 8, 11, 15, 17
(C) 6, 10, 14, 18　　(D) 8, 11, 14, 17

5. Write the next 3 numbers in the following pattern.

30, 32, 34, _____, _____, _____

(A) 36, 38, 40　　(B) 34, 36, 38
(C) 36, 40, 44　　(D) None of these

6. Thick is related to Thin in the same way as Idle is related to _______.
(A) Virtuous　　(B) Business
(C) Industrious　　(D) Activity

7. Coherent is related to Consistent in the same way as Irate is related to _______.
(A) Unreasonable　　(B) Unhappy
(C) Irritated　　(D) Angry

8. Claymore is related to Sword in the same way as Beretta is related to _______.
(A) Club　　(B) Axe
(C) Knife　　(D) Gun

9. Lion is related to Prowl in the same way as Bear is related to _______.
(A) Frisk　　(B) Lumber
(C) Stride　　(D) Bound

10. Mirror is related to Reflection in the same way as Water is related to _______.
(A) Conduction　　(B) Dispersion
(C) Immersion　　(D) Refraction

Direction (11–15): Find the next letter in the series given below.

11. C D E F G ?
(A) K　　(B) J
(C) I　　(D) H

12. A D G J M ?
(A) O　　(B) P
(C) Q　　(D) R

13. D F H J L ?
(A) O　　(B) N
(C) M　　(D) P

14. F G H I J ?
(A) N　　(B) L
(C) K　　(D) M

15. C E G I K ?
(A) M　　(B) N
(C) O　　(D) L

16. Find the odd one out.
(A) CD　　(B) KL
(C) EF　　(D) ON

17. Which one is different from the others?
(A) AC　　(B) TU
(C) MO　　(D) XZ

18. Identify the one that does not belong to the group.
(A) POP　　(B) BOB
(C) POT　　(D) TOT

19. Identify the one which is different from the others.
(A) CCD　　(B) FFG
(C) MMN　　(D) VVX

20. Find the odd one out.
(A) YSS　　(B) SYS
(C) SXS　　(D) SSY

21. If GO = 32, SHE = 49, then SOME will be equal to _______.
(A) 56　　(B) 58
(C) 62　　(D) 64

22. If ZIP = 30 and ZAP = 38, what will be VIP = ?
(A) 174　　(B) 43
(C) 34　　(D) 113

23. In a certain language, the numbers are coded as follows:

4	3	9	2	1	6	7	8	5	2	0
A	W	P	Q	R	B	E	S	G	J	M

How is the following number coded in that code?

421665

(A) AQRBBG   (B) PQBRSE
(C) ASGRBE   (D) QRPSSE

24. If bat is racket, racket is football, football is shuttle, shuttle is ludo and ludo is carrom, what is cricket played with?
(A) Racket   (B) Football
(C) Bat   (D) Shuttle

25. If banana is apple, apple is grapes, grapes is mango, mango is nuts, nuts is guava, which of the following is a yellow fruit?
(A) Mango   (B) Guava
(C) Apple   (D) Nuts

26. Some boys are sitting in a row. P is sitting fourteenth from the left and Q is seventh from the right. If there are four boys between P and Q, how many boys are there in the row?
(A) 19   (B) 21
(C) 23   (D) 25

27. Golu is 7 ranks ahead of Ankit in a class of 39. If Ankit's rank is seventeenth from the last, what is Golu's rank from the start?
(A) 11th   (B) 13th
(C) 16th   (D) 18th

28. Meetu is fourteenth from the right end in a row of 40 boys. What is his position from the left end?
(A) 21th   (B) 24th
(C) 25th   (D) 27th

29. In a row of trees, one tree is fifth from either end of the row. How many trees are there in the row?
(A) 8   (B) 9
(C) 10   (D) 11

30. In a class of 35 students, Kamal is placed seventh from the bottom where as Sunil is placed ninth from the top. Manoj is placed exactly in between the two. What is Kamal's position from Manoj?
(A) 7th   (B) 9th
(C) 10th   (D) 12th

31. Choose the alternative which closely resembles the mirror image of the given combination.

TERMINATE
(1) TƎᴚMIИATƎ   (2) ƎTAИIMᴚƎT
(3) ƎTAИIMᴚƎT   (4) ETAИIMᴚƎT
(A) 1   (B) 2
(C) 3   (D) 4

32. Choose the alternative which closely resembles the mirror image of the given combination.

BRISK
(1) ꓘSIᴚB   (2) ꓘƨIᴚB
(3) ꓘƨIᴚB   (4) ꓘSIᴚB
(A) 1   (B) 2
(C) 3   (D) 4

33. Choose the alternative which closely resembles the mirror image of the given combination.

INFORMATIONS
(1) IИⱭOᴚMAꓕIOИƨ   (2) IИⱵOᴚMATIOИƨ
(3) ƨИOITAMᴚOⱵИI   (4) ƨИOITAWᴚOⱵИI
(A) 1   (B) 2
(C) 3   (D) 4

34. Choose the alternative which closely resembles the mirror image of the given combination.

FIXING
(1) GИIXIF   (2) ⱵIXIИⱭ
(3) ⱭИIXIF   (4) ⱭИIXIⱵ
(A) 1   (B) 2
(C) 3   (D) 4

35. Choose the alternative which closely resembles the mirror image of the given combination.

WHITE
(1) ƎTIHW   (2) ƎTIHM
(3) ƎTIHW   (4) ETIHW
(A) 1   (B) 2
(C) 3   (D) 4

Directions (36 – 40): In each of the following questions, find out which of the answer figures (A), (B), (C) and (D) completes the figure matrix?

36. Select a suitable figure from the four alternatives to make the figure matrix complete.

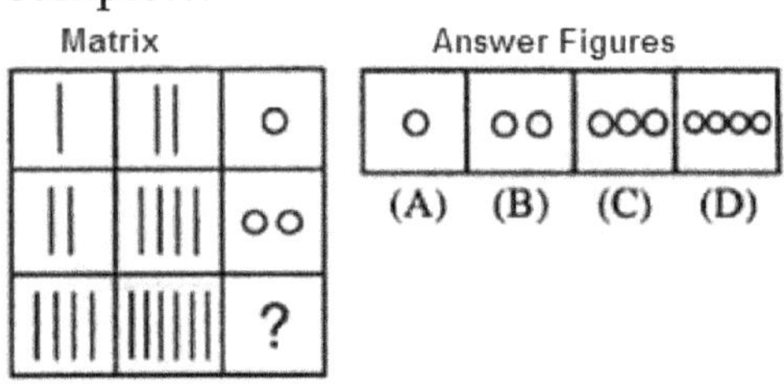

(A) A   (B) B
(C) C   (D) D

37. Select a suitable figure from the four alternatives to make the figure matrix complete.

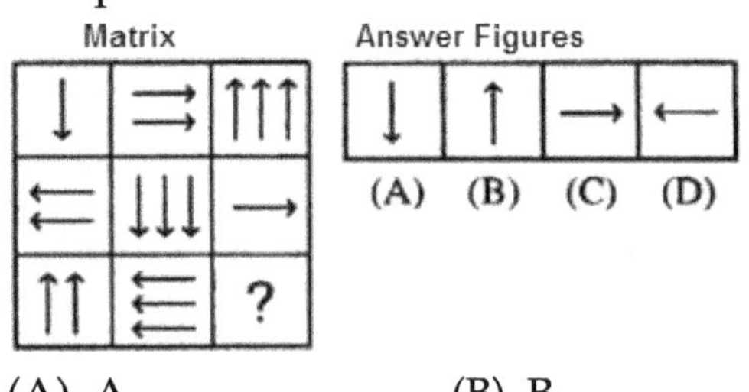

(A) A   (B) B
(C) C   (D) D

38. Select a suitable figure from the four alternatives to make the figure matrix complete.

(A) A   (B) B
(C) C   (D) D

39. Select a suitable figure from the four alternatives to make the figure matrix complete.

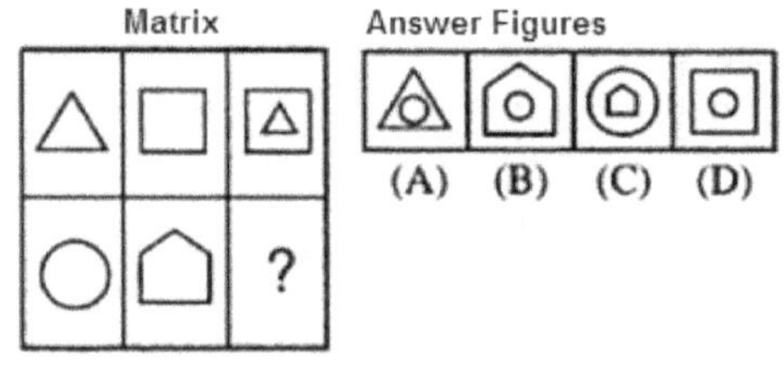

(A) A   (B) B
(C) C   (D) D

40. Select a suitable figure from the four alternatives to make the figure matrix complete.

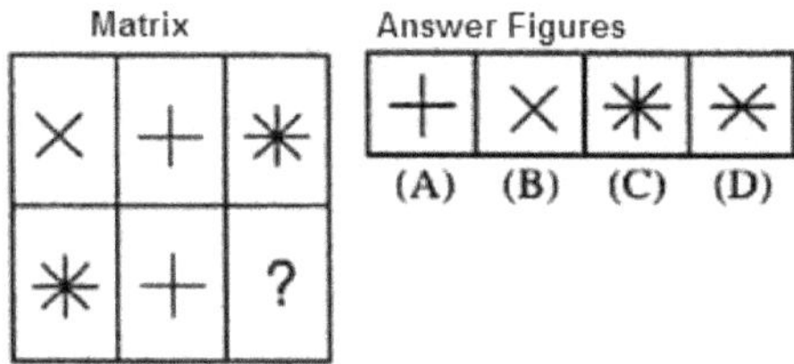

(A) A   (B) B
(C) C   (D) D

41. What is the shape of the tissue box?

(A) Triangle   (B) Rectangle
(C) Square   (D) Circle

42. What is the shape of the STOP sign?

(A) Hexagon   (B) Octagon
(C) Pentagon   (D) Sphere

43. What is the shape of the globe?

(A) Triangle   (B) Square
(C) Circle   (D) Rectangle

44. What is the shape of the buildings and yield sign?

(A) Rectangle and square
(B) Triangle and rectangle
(C) Cube and triangle
(D) Rectangular pyramid and triangle

45. Which shapes are used to draw the house shown in the figure?

(A) Square, triangle, and rectangle
(B) Square, circle, and rectangle
(C) Square, triangle, and hexagon
(D) Square, triangle, and circle

46. If brushing : minutes : : sleeping : ?
(A) Seconds   (B) Hours
(C) Days   (C) Months

47. Find the odd one out.
(A) 10/ 11/ 2001
(B) 5/ 17/ 2001
(C) 17/ 5/ 2001
(D) 11/ 10/ 2001

48. AM refers to which part of the day?
(A) Morning   (B) Afternoon
(C) Evening   (D) Lunchtime

49. The sun is at its peak at what time of the day?
(A) Morning   (B) Noon
(C) Evening   (D) Night

50. Moon shines brightly at ________.
(A) Morning   (B) Noon
(C) Evening   (D) Night

1. Ⓐ Ⓑ Ⓒ Ⓓ	11. Ⓐ Ⓑ Ⓒ Ⓓ	21. Ⓐ Ⓑ Ⓒ Ⓓ	31 Ⓐ Ⓑ Ⓒ Ⓓ	41. Ⓐ Ⓑ Ⓒ Ⓓ
2. Ⓐ Ⓑ Ⓒ Ⓓ	12. Ⓐ Ⓑ Ⓒ Ⓓ	22. Ⓐ Ⓑ Ⓒ Ⓓ	32. Ⓐ Ⓑ Ⓒ Ⓓ	42. Ⓐ Ⓑ Ⓒ Ⓓ
3. Ⓐ Ⓑ Ⓒ Ⓓ	13. Ⓐ Ⓑ Ⓒ Ⓓ	23. Ⓐ Ⓑ Ⓒ Ⓓ	33. Ⓐ Ⓑ Ⓒ Ⓓ	43. Ⓐ Ⓑ Ⓒ Ⓓ
4. Ⓐ Ⓑ Ⓒ Ⓓ	14. Ⓐ Ⓑ Ⓒ Ⓓ	24. Ⓐ Ⓑ Ⓒ Ⓓ	34. Ⓐ Ⓑ Ⓒ Ⓓ	44. Ⓐ Ⓑ Ⓒ Ⓓ
5. Ⓐ Ⓑ Ⓒ Ⓓ	15. Ⓐ Ⓑ Ⓒ Ⓓ	25. Ⓐ Ⓑ Ⓒ Ⓓ	35. Ⓐ Ⓑ Ⓒ Ⓓ	45. Ⓐ Ⓑ Ⓒ Ⓓ
6. Ⓐ Ⓑ Ⓒ Ⓓ	16. Ⓐ Ⓑ Ⓒ Ⓓ	26. Ⓐ Ⓑ Ⓒ Ⓓ	36. Ⓐ Ⓑ Ⓒ Ⓓ	46. Ⓐ Ⓑ Ⓒ Ⓓ
7. Ⓐ Ⓑ Ⓒ Ⓓ	17. Ⓐ Ⓑ Ⓒ Ⓓ	27. Ⓐ Ⓑ Ⓒ Ⓓ	37. Ⓐ Ⓑ Ⓒ Ⓓ	47. Ⓐ Ⓑ Ⓒ Ⓓ
8. Ⓐ Ⓑ Ⓒ Ⓓ	18. Ⓐ Ⓑ Ⓒ Ⓓ	28. Ⓐ Ⓑ Ⓒ Ⓓ	38. Ⓐ Ⓑ Ⓒ Ⓓ	48. Ⓐ Ⓑ Ⓒ Ⓓ
9. Ⓐ Ⓑ Ⓒ Ⓓ	19. Ⓐ Ⓑ Ⓒ Ⓓ	29. Ⓐ Ⓑ Ⓒ Ⓓ	39. Ⓐ Ⓑ Ⓒ Ⓓ	49. Ⓐ Ⓑ Ⓒ Ⓓ
10. Ⓐ Ⓑ Ⓒ Ⓓ	20. Ⓐ Ⓑ Ⓒ Ⓓ	30. Ⓐ Ⓑ Ⓒ Ⓓ	40. Ⓐ Ⓑ Ⓒ Ⓓ	50. Ⓐ Ⓑ Ⓒ Ⓓ

MODEL TEST PAPER

1. Look at this series: 7, 10, 8, 11, 9, 12, ... Which number should come next?
   (A) 7 (B) 10
   (C) 12 (D) 13

2. Identify the figure that completes the pattern given in figure (x).

   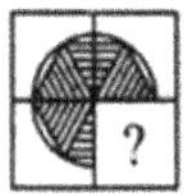    

   (X) (1) (2) (3) (4)
   (A) 1 (B) 2
   (C) 3 (D) 4

3. Mirror image of MOUTH is __________.
   (A) HTUOM (B) TUMOH
   (C) HTMOU (D) MOUTH

4. If A + B means A is the mother of B; A – B means A is the brother B; A % B means A is the father of B and A × B means A is the sister of B, which of the following shows that P is the maternal uncle of Q?
   (A) $Q - N + M \times P$ (B) $P + S \times N - Q$
   (C) $P - M + N \times Q$ (D) $Q - S \% P$

5. If South-East becomes North, North-East becomes West and so on. What will West become?
   (A) North-East (B) North-West
   (C) South-East (D) South-West

6. Seeds are not used for reproduction in __________.
   (A) Lemons (B) Potatoes
   (C) Tomatoes (D) Jowar

7. Classify mango, coconut, rambutan, arecanut, according to the branching of stem: branched trunk; unbranched trunk.
   (A) Mango, rambutan; coconut, arecanut
   (B) Coconut, arecanut; mango, rambutan
   (C) Mango, arecanut; coconut, rambutan
   (D) Coconut, rambutan; mango, arecanut

8. If a squirrel was added to this diagram, it would be on the same tropic level as the __________.

   (A) Bird (B) Snake
   (C) Mouse (D) Mushroom

9. Which of the following animals swallows its food as whole?
   (A) Snake (B) Cat
   (C) Dog (D) Wolf

10. Which of the following spins webs to trap insects and eat them?
    (A) Butterfly (B) Spider
    (C) Fireflies (D) Honey bees

11. Look at the given classification table. Which of the following can Q be?

Body System	
Heart: Blood vessels	Lungs: Q

    (A) Brain (B) Nose
    (C) Intestine (D) Backbone

12. Look at the following activities. In which of these activities, the heart would pump faster to transport the oxygen to the cells?

(A) 

(B) 

(C) 

(D) All of these

13. Refer the given figures showing different types of bird's feet and answer the questions.

I. **Which of these bird feets is suitable for climbing and clinging to the bark of tree?**

II. **Which of these bird feets has talons?**

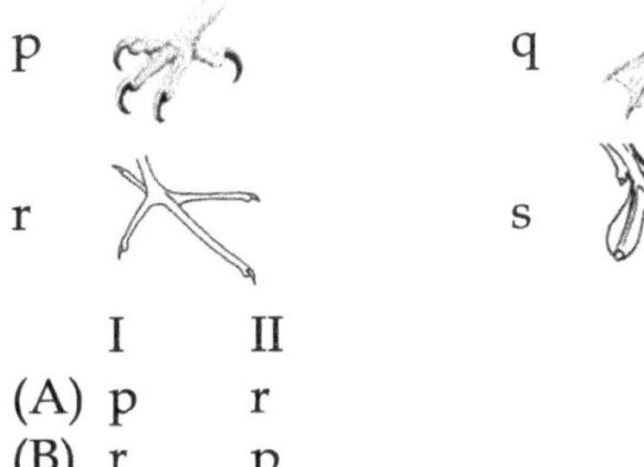

	I	II
(A)	p	r
(B)	r	p
(C)	q	s
(D)	s	r

14. Water drops from the sky as rain. Where does all this water go?
   i.   It collects into the ponds and reservoirs.
   ii. It is absorbed by the ground.
   iii. It flows into the rivers and streams.
   iv. The plants absorb the water.
   (A) i, ii and iii   (B) i and ii
   (C) i and iv   (D) All of these

15. _________ is a process in the water cycle, in which the water vapour rises into the atmosphere.
   (A) Precipitation   (B) Transpiration
   (C) Condensation   (D) Evaporation

16. When a scoop of ice cream is left under the sun for an hour, there is a change in its _________.
   i.   State
   ii. Mass
   iii. Volume
   (A) i & iii only   (B) i & ii only
   (C) ii & iii only   (D) i, ii and iii

17. Ananya is doing an experiment. She puts some ice cubes on a jar as shown in the figure. The jar was empty at the beginning of the experiment. But after sometime she observes water inside the jar. The water is a result of _________ of ice cubes.

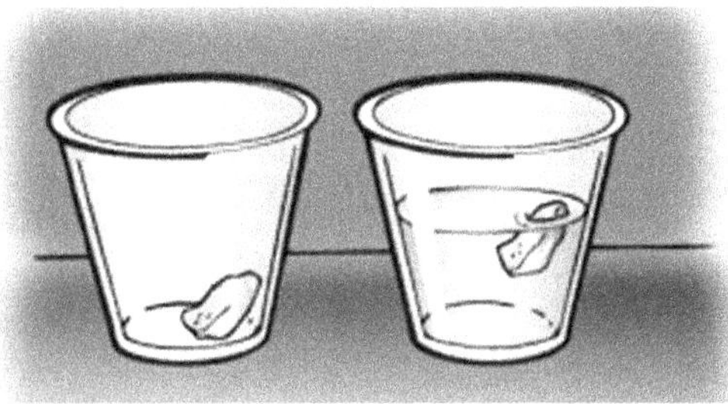

   (A) Melting
   (B) Evaporation
   (C) Freezing
   (D) Both (A) and (B)

18. Study the given classification chart carefully. An object P can be placed under both groups. What could the object P be made of?

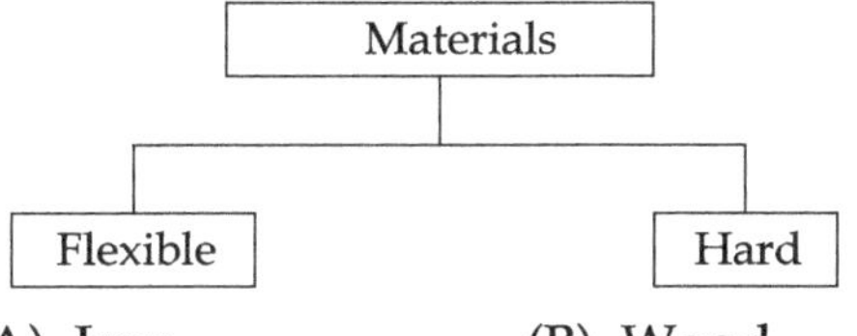

   (A) Iron   (B) Wood
   (C) Plastic   (D) Glass

19. Matter that is liquid tends to be denser than matter that is _________.
   (A) Gas   (B) Solid
   (C) Liquid   (D) Matter

20. Which of the following food items are protein-rich?

i.

ii.

iii.

iv.

v.

(A) i, ii, and iii
(B) ii, iii and iv
(C) iii and v
(D) i, ii, iii and v

21. The oil extracted from which of the following food items can be used for cooking?
(A) coconut
(B) groundnut
(C) mustard
(D) All of these

22. Vehicle 'X' is not owned by us. We have to pay to travel by 'X'.
I.   Select an example of 'X' vehicle?
II. Which of the 'X' vehicles can run on rail tracks laid on road?

	I	II
(A)	Ship	Scooter
(B)	Motorcycle	Metro
(C)	Airplane	Tram
(D)	Bicycle	Cable car

23. Which of the following transports is used to carry more than 35 passengers?
(A) Truck
(B) Car
(C) Bus
(D) Auto rickshaw

24. Select the option in which the correct odd one is encircled.
(A) Car, bus, Scooter, bullock, cart
(B) Cycle, car, airplane, train
(C) Airplane, hot air balloon, Helicopter, boat
(D) Ship, Submarine, car, Boat

25. Match the following and choose the correct option:

	I		II
a.	Fire engine	i.	Carry people in deserts
b.	Camels	ii.	Carry patient
c.	Ambulance	iii.	Equipped to put off fire
d.	Postal van	iv.	Carry police men
e.	Police van	v.	Carry letters

(A) a-iii, b-i, c-ii, d-v, e-iv
(B) a-i, b- iii, c-ii, d-v, e-iv
(C) a-i, b- iii, c-v, d-iv, e-ii
(D) a-i, b- iii, c-ii, d-iv, e-v

26. What is happening in the following picture?

(A) A moving ball is stopped by placing the leg before it.
(B) The direction of the ball is changed with the bat.
(C) There is an increase in the speed of a moving body.
(D) There is a decrease in the speed of a moving object.

27. Which kind of energy is produced when a person beats a drum?
(A) Electrical
(B) Sound
(C) Light
(D) Chemical

28. Electricity traveling through a wire is an example of __________.
(A) A force applied by a simple machine.
(B) Energy flowing through the water cycle.

OLYMPIAD WORKBOOK (NSO) CLASS – 3

(C) Earth's gravitational pull on an object.
(D) Energy being transferred from one place to another.

29. Which cycle is correct?
(A) Morning - Sunrise - Afternoon - Sunset
(B) Summer - Fall - Winter - Spring
(C) Seed - Fruit - Seedling
(B) Baby - Child - Teenager - Adult

30. These planets have rings __________.
(A) Mars, Jupiter and Saturn
(B) Saturn, Pluto, Neptune and Venus
(C) Jupiter, Saturn, Uranus and Neptune
(D) Jupiter, Saturn, Neptune and Venus

31. While exercising, our body needs more oxygen. Which of the following systems ensures that our body receives enough oxygen?

P - Respiratory system

Q - Digestive system

R - Circulatory system

(A) P only
(B) Q only
(C) P and R only
(D) Q and R only

32. Look at the given classification table. Which of the following can 'X' be?

Body Systems	
Lungs : Nose	Heart : 'X'

(A) Small Intestine
(B) Backbone
(C) Brain
(D) Blood vessels

33. What do the items given have in common?

(i) They can be found on a seedling.
(ii) They are fruits.
(iii) They come from flowering plants.
(iv) They have seeds.
(A) Only (iii) and (iv)
(B) Only (i), (iii) and (iv)
(C) Only (ii), (iii) and (iv)
(D) (i), (ii), (iii) and (iv)

34. On a hot summer day, Radha kept the same amount of water in 4 containers in the kitchen. After a few hours, water in which container will be coldest?
(A) A plastic bottle
(B) A steel vessel
(C) A mud pot
(D) A glass bottle

35. The figure given shows a group of stars. Which of the following terms is used to describe the group of stars?

(A) Purnima
(B) Constellation
(C) Galaxy
(D) Orbit

—Darken Your Choice with HB Pencil—

1.	Ⓐ Ⓑ Ⓒ Ⓓ	8.	Ⓐ Ⓑ Ⓒ Ⓓ	15.	Ⓐ Ⓑ Ⓒ Ⓓ	22	Ⓐ Ⓑ Ⓒ Ⓓ	29.	Ⓐ Ⓑ Ⓒ Ⓓ
2.	Ⓐ Ⓑ Ⓒ Ⓓ	9.	Ⓐ Ⓑ Ⓒ Ⓓ	16.	Ⓐ Ⓑ Ⓒ Ⓓ	23.	Ⓐ Ⓑ Ⓒ Ⓓ	30.	Ⓐ Ⓑ Ⓒ Ⓓ
3.	Ⓐ Ⓑ Ⓒ Ⓓ	10.	Ⓐ Ⓑ Ⓒ Ⓓ	17.	Ⓐ Ⓑ Ⓒ Ⓓ	24.	Ⓐ Ⓑ Ⓒ Ⓓ	31.	Ⓐ Ⓑ Ⓒ Ⓓ
4.	Ⓐ Ⓑ Ⓒ Ⓓ	11.	Ⓐ Ⓑ Ⓒ Ⓓ	18.	Ⓐ Ⓑ Ⓒ Ⓓ	25.	Ⓐ Ⓑ Ⓒ Ⓓ	32.	Ⓐ Ⓑ Ⓒ Ⓓ
5.	Ⓐ Ⓑ Ⓒ Ⓓ	12.	Ⓐ Ⓑ Ⓒ Ⓓ	19.	Ⓐ Ⓑ Ⓒ Ⓓ	26.	Ⓐ Ⓑ Ⓒ Ⓓ	33.	Ⓐ Ⓑ Ⓒ Ⓓ
6.	Ⓐ Ⓑ Ⓒ Ⓓ	13.	Ⓐ Ⓑ Ⓒ Ⓓ	20.	Ⓐ Ⓑ Ⓒ Ⓓ	27.	Ⓐ Ⓑ Ⓒ Ⓓ	34.	Ⓐ Ⓑ Ⓒ Ⓓ
7.	Ⓐ Ⓑ Ⓒ Ⓓ	14.	Ⓐ Ⓑ Ⓒ Ⓓ	21.	Ⓐ Ⓑ Ⓒ Ⓓ	28.	Ⓐ Ⓑ Ⓒ Ⓓ	35.	Ⓐ Ⓑ Ⓒ Ⓓ

HINTS AND SOLUTIONS

1. PLANTS AND ANIMALS

Answer Key

1. (A)	2. (D)	3. (C)	4. (B)	5. (C)	6. (C)	7. (A)	8. (A)	9. (D)	10. (C)
11. (D)	12. (B)	13. (B)	14. (A)	15. (A)	16. (A)	17. (C)	18. (A)	19. (C)	20. (C)
21. (B)	22. (D)	23. (D)	24. (D)	25. (C)	26. (D)	27. (C)	28. (C)	29. (A)	30. (D)

HOTS (ACHIEVERS SECTION)

31. (D)	32. (B)	33. (B)	34. (C)	35. (C)

2. BIRDS

Answer Key

1. (A)	2. (C)	3. (B)	4. (A)	5. (C)	6. (D)	7. (D)	8. (D)	9. (D)	10. (A)
11. (B)	12. (B)	13. (B)	14. (A)	15. (A)	16. (A)	17. (A)	18. (C)	19. (A)	20. (A)
21. (A)	22. (C)	23. (C)	24. (D)	25. (C)	26. (A)	27. (A)	28. (A)	29. (A)	30. (D)

HOTS (ACHIEVERS SECTION)

31. (A)	32. (C)	33. (A)	34. (C)	35. (C)

3. FOOD

Answer Key

1. (D)	2. (A)	3. (D)	4. (B)	5. (D)	6. (D)	7. (C)	8. (C)	9. (A)	10. (D)
11. (A)	12. (B)	13. (A)	14. (B)	15. (D)	16. (D)	17. (C)	18. (C)	19. (C)	20. (B)
21. (A)	22. (A)	23. (D)	24. (B)	25. (A)	26. (B)	27. (D)	28. (C)	29. (A)	30. (A)

HOTS (ACHIEVERS SECTION)

31. (D)	32. (D)	33. (C)	34. (D)	35. (B)

4. HOUSING, CLOTHING AND OCCUPATION

Answer Key

1. (C)	2. (A)	3. (D)	4. (D)	5. (A)	6. (A)	7. (A)	8. (C)	9. (B)	10. (A)
11. (A)	12. (D)	13. (D)	14. (B)	15. (D)	16. (B)	17. (A)	18. (B)	19. (D)	20. (A)
21. (C)	22. (A)	23. (C)	24. (B)	25. (B)	26. (C)	27. (D)	28. (B)	29. (C)	30. (D)

HOTS (ACHIEVERS SECTION)

31. (B)	32. (B)	33. (D)	34. (D)	35. (C)

5. TRANSPORT AND COMMUNICATION

Answer Key

1. (B)	2. (B)	3. (C)	4. (C)	5. (C)	6. (C)	7. (B)	8. (B)	9. (C)	10. (C)
11. (B)	12. (B)	13. (B)	14. (B)	15. (A)	16. (D)	17. (C)	18. (D)	19. (B)	20. (A)
21. (A)	22. (B)	23. (A)	24. (A)	25. (A)	26. (B)	27. (D)	28. (D)	29. (C)	30. (C)

HOTS (ACHIEVERS SECTION)

31. (A)	32. (C)	33. (A)	34. (D)	35. (D)

6. HUMAN BODY

Answer Key

1. (A)	2. (C)	3. (D)	4. (D)	5. (B)	6. (C)	7. (C)	8. (B)	9. (C)	10. (A)
11. (B)	12. (B)	13. (C)	14. (A)	15. (C)	16. (B)	17. (D)	18. (C)	19. (B)	20. (C)
21. (C)	22. (B)	23. (D)	24. (C)	25. (B)					

HOTS (ACHIEVERS SECTION)

26. (C)	27. (C)	28. (A)	29. (B)	30. (C)

7. EARTH AND UNIVERSE

Answer Key

1. (B)	2. (A)	3. (C)	4. (B)	5. (D)	6. (C)	7. (D)	8. (B)	9. (A)	10. (D)
11. (C)	12. (D)	13. (B)	14. (A)	15. (B)	16. (C)	17. (A)	18. (A)	19. (B)	20. (C)
21. (D)	22. (C)	23. (A)	24. (C)	25. (C)	26. (A)	27. (C)	28. (B)	29. (B)	30. (B)

HOTS (ACHIEVERS SECTION)

31. (C)	32. (C)	33. (A)	34. (D)	35. (A)

8. MATTER AND MATERIALS

Answer Key

1. (C)	2. (C)	3. (A)	4. (A)	5. (B)	6. (A)	7. (B)	8. (D)	9. (D)	10. (C)
11. (B)	12. (A)	13. (D)	14. (C)	15. (C)	16. (A)	17. (D)	18. (A)	19. (A)	20. (B)
21. (B)	22. (A)	23. (D)	24. (A)	25. (C)	26. (D)	27. (B)	28. (A)	29. (C)	30. (B)

HOTS (ACHIEVERS SECTION)

31. (D)	32. (D)	33. (D)	34. (A)	35. (D)

9. LIGHT, FORCE AND SOUND

Answer Key

1. (B)	2. (D)	3. (C)	4. (A)	5. (C)	6. (C)	7. (B)	8. (D)	9. (D)	10. (B)
11. (D)	12. (C)	13. (B)	14. (B)	15. (B)	16. (C)	17. (B)	18. (D)	19. (B)	20. (D)
21. (D)	22. (C)	23. (B)	24. (C)	25. (C)					

HOTS (ACHIEVERS SECTION)

26. (B)	27. (B)	28. (D)	29. (D)	30. (B)

10. OUR ENVIRONMENT

Answer Key

1. (A)	2. (C)	3. (A)	4. (D)	5. (B)	6. (D)	7. (A)	8. (B)	9. (C)	10. (A)
11. (D)	12. (D)	13. (A)	14. (D)	15. (B)	16. (A)	17. (B)	18. (D)	19. (D)	20. (C)

16. **(A)**
Pollution is the process of making land, water, air or other parts of the environment dirty and not safe or suitable to use. This can be done through the introduction of a contaminant into a natural environment, but the contaminant doesn't need to be tangible.

17. **(B)**
The substance which produces pollution is called as pollutants. Pollutant may be the man made like smoke and natural like forest fire.

18. **(D)**
There are different types of pollution: water pollution, air pollution, solid

waste pollution and noise pollution. All of these can be found in urban areas. The main sources of pollution are household activities, factories, agriculture and transport.

19. (D)

Earth's atmosphere is composed of about 78 percent nitrogen, 21 percent oxygen, 0.9 percent argon, and 0.1 percent other gases. Trace amounts of carbon dioxide, methane, water vapor, and neon are some of the other gases that make up the remaining 0.1 percent.

20. (C)

Air Pollution – The crackers contains many toxic gases and chemical compounds which activates after getting in touch with exposed air and start harming us. Example Nitrous oxide, which remains in air for long time if the area doesn't get heavy rain or strong winds. Cigarette smoking causes environmental pollution by releasing toxic air pollutants into the atmosphere. The cigarette butts also litter the environment, and the toxic chemicals in the residues seep into soils and waterways, thereby causing soil and water pollution, respectively.

HOTS (ACHIEVERS SECTION)

21. (A)	22. (B)	23. (D)	24. (D)	25. (B)

1. (A)

Through a process called photosynthesis, leaves pull in carbon dioxide and water and use the energy of the sun to convert this into chemical compounds such as sugars that feed the tree. But as a by-product of that chemical reaction oxygen is produced and released by the tree.

2. (B)

Other activities, including cutting down trees, also emit greenhouse gases. The high concentration of these greenhouse gases in the atmosphere is responsible for increasing more heat on Earth, which leads to an increase in global temperature. Climate scientists believe that human activities are the main reason behind global warming.

3. (D)

Water pollution is the release of substances into bodies of water that makes water unsafe for human use and disrupts aquatic ecosystems. Water pollution can be caused by a plethora of different contaminants, including toxic waste, petroleum, and disease-causing microorganisms.

4. (D)

You need water to digest your food and get rid of waste. Water is needed for digestive juices, urine (pee), and poop. And you can bet that water is the main ingredient in perspiration, also called sweat. Besides being an important part of the fluids in your body, water is needed by each cell to work.

5. (A)

Whenever we hear very loud noise it cause irritation. Noise annoyance can result from interference with daily activities, feelings, thoughts, sleep, or rest, and may be accompanied by negative emotional responses, such as irritability, distress, exhaustion, a wish to escape the noise and other stress-related symptoms.

Answer Key

1. (A)	2. (B)	3. (C)	4. (D)	5. (A)	6. (C)	7. (D)	8. (D)	9. (B)	10. (D)
11. (D)	12. (B)	13. (B)	14. (C)	15. (A)	16. (D)	17. (B)	18. (C)	19. (D)	20. (C)
21. (A)	22. (C)	23. (A)	24. (A)	25. (D)	26. (D)	27. (C)	28. (D)	29. (B)	30. (C)
31. (C)	32. (D)	33. (C)	34. (D)	35. (C)	36. (D)	37. (C)	38. (A)	39. (B)	40. (B)
41. (B)	42. (B)	43. (C)	44. (B)	45. (A)	46. (B)	47. (B)	48. (A)	49. (B)	50. (D)

6. (C)
The words in each pair are antonyms of each other.

7. (D)
The words in each pair are synonyms.

8. (D)
The first is a type of the second.

9. (B)
The second is the manner of walking of the first.

10. (D)
Light rays falling on a mirror undergo reflection and those falling on water undergo refraction.

11. (D)
The pattern of the series is:
$$C \xrightarrow{+1} D \xrightarrow{+1} E \xrightarrow{+1} F \xrightarrow{+1} G \xrightarrow{+1} \boxed{H}$$
$\therefore ? = H$

12. (B)
The pattern of the series is:
$$A \xrightarrow{+3} D \xrightarrow{+3} G \xrightarrow{+3} J \xrightarrow{+3} M \xrightarrow{+3} \boxed{P}$$
$\therefore ? = P$

15. (A)
The pattern of the series is:
$$C \xrightarrow{+2} E \xrightarrow{+2} G \xrightarrow{+2} I \xrightarrow{+2} R \xrightarrow{+2} \boxed{L}$$
$\therefore ? = L$

16. (D)
Here $C \xrightarrow{+1} D$, $K \xrightarrow{+1} L$, $E \xrightarrow{+1} F$ but
$O \xrightarrow{+1} N$
$\therefore$ D is Correct answer.

18. (C)

Here $\overset{\frown}{P \ O \ P}$ $\overset{\frown}{B \ O \ B}$ $P \ O \ T$ $\overset{\frown}{T \ O \ T}$
Clearly P O T is different

19 (D)
First two letters are same and then comes next letter. Clearly VVX is different. VVW (according to pattern)

26. (D)
Number of boys in the row = number of boys till P + number of boys between P and Q + number of boys including Q and those behind Q = 14 + 4 + 7 = 25.

27. (C)
Ankit is 17th from the last and Golu is 7 ranks ahead of Ankit. So, Golu is 24th from the last. Number of students ahead of Golu in rank = (39 – 24) = 15. So, Golu is 16th from the start.

28. (D)
Clearly, number of boys towards the Meetu's left = (40 – 14) = 26. So, Meetu is 27th from the left end.

29. (B)
Clearly number of trees in the row
= (4 + 1 + 4) = 9.

30. (C)
Number of students between Kamal and Sunil = 35 – (7 + 9) = 19. Clearly, there are 9 students between Kamal and Manoj, as well as Manoj and Sunil. So, Kamal is 10th from Manoj.

Answer Key

1. (B)	2. (C)	3. (A)	4. (C)	5. (C)	6. (B)	7. (A)	8. (C)	9. (A)	10. (B)
11. (B)	12. (D)	13. (A)	14. (D)	15. (D)	16. (D)	17. (A)	18. (C)	19. (A)	20. (C)
21. (D)	22. (C)	23. (C)	24. (B)	25. (A)	26. (B)	27. (B)	28. (D)	29. (D)	30. (C)
31. (C)	32. (D)	33. (C)	34. (C)	35. (B)					

SAMPLE OMR ANSWER SHEET

1. STUDENT NAME (IN ENGLISH CAPITAL LETTERS ONLY)

Students must write and darken the respective circles completely using HB Pencil only. Othewise their Answer Sheets will not be evaluated.

PERSONAL DETAILS

2. SCHOOL CODE

3. CLASS

4. SECTION

5. ROLL NO.

6. QUESTION PAPER SET

A ○
B ○
C ○
D ○

7. MOBILE NUMBER

8. GENDER

MALE ○
FEMALE ○

9. STREAM
(Only for Class XI and XII Students)

MATHEMATICS ○
BIOLOGY ○
OTHERS ○

MARK YOUR ANSWERS

1.	Ⓐ Ⓑ Ⓒ Ⓓ	26.	Ⓐ Ⓑ Ⓒ Ⓓ
2.	Ⓐ Ⓑ Ⓒ Ⓓ	27.	Ⓐ Ⓑ Ⓒ Ⓓ
3.	Ⓐ Ⓑ Ⓒ Ⓓ	28.	Ⓐ Ⓑ Ⓒ Ⓓ
4.	Ⓐ Ⓑ Ⓒ Ⓓ	29.	Ⓐ Ⓑ Ⓒ Ⓓ
5.	Ⓐ Ⓑ Ⓒ Ⓓ	30.	Ⓐ Ⓑ Ⓒ Ⓓ
6.	Ⓐ Ⓑ Ⓒ Ⓓ	31.	Ⓐ Ⓑ Ⓒ Ⓓ
7.	Ⓐ Ⓑ Ⓒ Ⓓ	32.	Ⓐ Ⓑ Ⓒ Ⓓ
8.	Ⓐ Ⓑ Ⓒ Ⓓ	33.	Ⓐ Ⓑ Ⓒ Ⓓ
9.	Ⓐ Ⓑ Ⓒ Ⓓ	34.	Ⓐ Ⓑ Ⓒ Ⓓ
10.	Ⓐ Ⓑ Ⓒ Ⓓ	35.	Ⓐ Ⓑ Ⓒ Ⓓ
11.	Ⓐ Ⓑ Ⓒ Ⓓ	36.	Ⓐ Ⓑ Ⓒ Ⓓ
12.	Ⓐ Ⓑ Ⓒ Ⓓ	37.	Ⓐ Ⓑ Ⓒ Ⓓ
13.	Ⓐ Ⓑ Ⓒ Ⓓ	38.	Ⓐ Ⓑ Ⓒ Ⓓ
14.	Ⓐ Ⓑ Ⓒ Ⓓ	39.	Ⓐ Ⓑ Ⓒ Ⓓ
15.	Ⓐ Ⓑ Ⓒ Ⓓ	40.	Ⓐ Ⓑ Ⓒ Ⓓ
16.	Ⓐ Ⓑ Ⓒ Ⓓ	41.	Ⓐ Ⓑ Ⓒ Ⓓ
17.	Ⓐ Ⓑ Ⓒ Ⓓ	42.	Ⓐ Ⓑ Ⓒ Ⓓ
18.	Ⓐ Ⓑ Ⓒ Ⓓ	43.	Ⓐ Ⓑ Ⓒ Ⓓ
19.	Ⓐ Ⓑ Ⓒ Ⓓ	44.	Ⓐ Ⓑ Ⓒ Ⓓ
20.	Ⓐ Ⓑ Ⓒ Ⓓ	45.	Ⓐ Ⓑ Ⓒ Ⓓ
21.	Ⓐ Ⓑ Ⓒ Ⓓ	46.	Ⓐ Ⓑ Ⓒ Ⓓ
22.	Ⓐ Ⓑ Ⓒ Ⓓ	47.	Ⓐ Ⓑ Ⓒ Ⓓ
23.	Ⓐ Ⓑ Ⓒ Ⓓ	48.	Ⓐ Ⓑ Ⓒ Ⓓ
24.	Ⓐ Ⓑ Ⓒ Ⓓ	49.	Ⓐ Ⓑ Ⓒ Ⓓ
25.	Ⓐ Ⓑ Ⓒ Ⓓ	50.	Ⓐ Ⓑ Ⓒ Ⓓ

Signature of the Student & Date of Examination

Signature of the Invigilator & Date of Examination